the free-spirited garDen

the free-spirited garden

Gorgeous Gardens That Flourish Naturally

by Susan McClure
With photographs by Ian Adams

CHRONICLE BOOKS
SAN FRANCISCO

Library of Congress Cataloging-in-Publication Data:
McClure, Susan, 1957-
The free-spirited garden : gorgeous gardens that flourish naturally / by Susan McClure ; photographs by Ian Adams.
        p. cm.
Includes index.
ISBN 0-8118-2112-9 (pbk.)
1. Natural landscaping. 2. Low maintenance gardening. I. Title.
SB439.M28 1999
635—dc21   97-49846
                                            CIP

Printed in Hong Kong.

Designed by Lisa Levin Design

Distributed in Canada by Raincoast Books
8680 Cambie Street
Vancouver, British Columbia V6P 6M9

10 9 8 7 6 5 4 3 2 1

Chronicle Books
85 Second Street
San Francisco, California 94105

www.chroniclebooks.com

To my father and attorney, John Adams, who is always there when I need him, and my husband, Ted, who enjoys wild areas and free-spirited gardens as much as I do.

My thanks must begin with people who opened their free-spirited gardens to my gifted photographer, Ian Adams, and myself. They include Trudi Temple, Don Vanderbrook, Valerie Strong, C. Coleston Burrell, Jim Hagstrom, Fred Rozumalski, Fred and Ranelle Brandt, Lorrie Otto, Ruth Stein, Kari Bunde, Janet Smedley, Eve Gardner, Diane and Kent Whealy, Ed and Donna Lambert, Susan Beard, Mary Versfelt, Madalene Hill and Gwen Barclay, Ron Lutsko, Carolee Snyder, Jim Adams, and the people at Crow Creek Mine.

Thanks also to the following who were kind enough to share special information: garden designer Edith Eddleman, daylily breeder Darell Apps, Lorrie Otto of Wild Ones, Judy Wigand of Judy's Perennials, Chris Dunn of Herban Gardens, Neil Diboll from Prairie Nursery, Dr. Benjamin Zamora from the University of Western Washington, Tom Johns from Territorial Seeds, Bill Thomas and Robert Armstrong from Longwood Gardens, Junie Hostetler of Native Seeds/SEARCH, and Michael Kost, naturalist for the Morton Arboretum.

My final applause is for my literary agents Charlotte Sheedy and Neeti Maddan, who handled the business end of this book so capably, and Leslie Jonath, an editor with a vision, who helped shape the book right from the start.

Contents

How to use this book.

The Free-Spirited Garden is devoted to flowers, herbs, and vegetables, and creative ideas for their use, some of which are sure to work well in your yard. To get the most from this book, it will be helpful to know the following specifics.

Seven different kinds of gardens are detailed in individual chapters, which feature descriptions and design ideas. Chapters end with a glossary of free-spirited plants. Favorite species are listed by common name, alphabetized by botanical name, and described according to growth habits, life cycle, usefulness, growing requirements, and more. Quick reference guides detail hardiness zones, companion plants, primary means of spreading, aggressiveness, and flowering time.

You will find botanical names occasionally listed in the text for certain key plants. These are species that aren't easily identified by the common name and aren't available in this book's glossaries. Knowing their botanical names will help you order or avoid them.

Under primary means of spreading, the generic term "creeping stems" indicates the presence of underground horizontal stems called rhizomes or aboveground creeping stems called stolons and runners. They all have similar anatomical origins and purposes but will be more or less visible depending on their position in or on the soil.

Mauve phlox and gloriosa daisies emerge on their own beside 'Autumn Joy' sedum.

CHAPTER 1:
what is a free-spirited garden?

In a free-spirited garden, a carefree blend of flowers, herbs, and vegetables reproduce themselves, arise impromptu from seeds, or spread into bold masses and drifts. The resulting riotous flower color and interwoven foliar tapestries—all produced with little extra effort on the part of the gardener—capture the ebb and flow of nature with plenty of excitement and surprises.

Self-seeding forget-me-nots surround a quiet pond.

Because free-spirited plants multiply without need for your help or money, they fit perfectly into modern lifestyles. Struggles to achieve computer-generated precision or to meet man-made standards for flawlessness are left behind. Instead of smothering spontaneity, you can enjoy the gifts of nature and soon find your garden blossoming into greater beauty and variety than man alone can impose.

A vivacious blend of self-sowing, rainbow-colored, peony-flowered poppies, silver-leaved rose champions, and purple foxgloves welcome visitors at a city cottage garden in Vancouver. In Valparaiso, Indiana, volunteer garden phlox, gloriosa daisies, and golden coneflowers pepper borders around an entire yard with sunny clusters of mauve and golden flowers. Elsewhere, airy purple-flowered inflorescences of verbena, petite crepe-petaled shirley poppies, and compact sprays of blue-flowered forget-me-nots arise between dull shrubs, spread along garden edges, and echo throughout the garden. These self-seeders create rhythm and continuity—strong design elements achieved simply by allowing well-placed seedlings to stay put.

Creeping perennials such as mother-of-thyme, barren strawberry, and bee balm form natural impromptu masses, the very thing gardeners hope to achieve when planting clusters of three, five, or seven nonmobile

16

'Golden Glow' cutleaf coneflower has creeping rhizomes that make it one of the most aggressively spreading coneflowers.

species. These natural spreaders can sweep around trees, cascade over walls, or unfurl into carpets. Where a lone small plant would be lost, they create a powerful effect with abundant flowers and foliage.

Free-spirited plants, whether self-seeders or spreaders, are natural opportunists. They find their own way to make an impression in the garden, needing no special coaxing, priming, primping, or man-made products to expand and multiply. They give the garden a natural, full, even frothy look and provide a handsome contrast to more controlled landscape elements—lawns, clipped shrubs, even the house itself.

Thyme spreads between stone steps.

But among the exuberant free-spirited plants are tyrants, and it is important to make a distinction between the two. Tyrannical spreaders, also called invasive or weedy plants, move so quickly and strongly that they consume entire gardens and choke out their neighbors. Plants like purple loosestrife (*Lythrum salicaria*), which has clogged wetlands across the eastern United States, and paperbark (*Melaleuca leucadendra*), an Australian tree that is gobbling acres of Florida wildlands, are too aggressive to set free, even in a free-spirited garden.

Most free-spirited plants, however, work on a smaller scale than those news-making tyrants. Spearmint, a vigorous creeper that moves on ground-hugging stems, can consume a yard of soil or more in a single growing season. Because any severed piece of creeping stem left in the soil will sprout into an aggressive new plant, it can be difficult to eradicate. Still, spearmint may merit planting in out-of-the-way places where it can spread freely without offense. Or it can be harnessed within containers, which set firm limits on its reach.

Your garden conditions will play a big part in how quickly free spirits spread. In one Boston-area garden, houttuynia, a beautiful perennial with red-, green-, and cream-colored leaves, stayed in a fairly contained sweep until the addition of irrigation. Once supplied with

Plant Reproduction and Diversity

With free-spirited gardening, it's important to recognize the inherent ability of plants to make their own contributions. Plants grow, flower, fruit, and seed, completing the natural cycles of life. In doing so, some move—not on legs but with airborne, animal-toted, or water-washed seeds or on creeping roots or stems.

Flowers are carefully orchestrated to ensure species survival and spread, elements of importance in free-spirited gardens. Colorful, fragrant, or nectar-rich blossoms entice bees, butterflies, and hummingbirds to visit and spread pollen from one flower to the next. Flowers may have special nectar-holding tubes, landing platforms for insect guests, or ultraviolet nectar guides pointing the way to a powdering of pollen to ensure the process is completed properly. The reward for this pollen-swapping process, called cross-pollination, is new genetic combinations and unique individuals arising in the next generation.

There is always a possibility that a cross-pollinated seedling will show up with a new feature, having extra cold hardiness, for example, which provides a survival advantage for the species. From the gardener's perspective, cross-pollinated seedlings offer the potential for larger flowers, new colors, different sizes, and other surprising and wonderful variations. Edith Eddleman, who is always watching for new developments, discovered a unique lavender-pink moss verbena (*Verbena tenuisecta*) seedling in her garden, named it 'Edith', and shared it with several nurseries that are offering it for sale. (For more on moss verbena, see page 113.)

Not all species emphasize the development of new and distinctive individuals. Some, such as Canadian goldenrod—a rambler able to stretch like waves of gold through prairies and meadows—also choose the more energy-efficient route of cloning. By cloning, free-spirited plants can spread with less flamboyance and more stealth on creeping roots or creeping stems such as underground rhizomes and aboveground stolons or runners, sprouting new mirror images of themselves as they go. Where ideally suited for the habitat, plant clones will do well. Where challenged, perhaps by drought or disease, they may not have the genetic flexibility to survive.

abundant moisture, it exploded through the garden and had to be removed.

The wily gardener can still enjoy some of the more rambunctious free-spirited plants if willing to manage them. Containing those that are inclined to run wild or removing faded flowers of aggressive seeders before the seeds mature can help maintain some order.

To learn the kind of mobility of a particular plant, consult aggressiveness notations in glossaries throughout this book. For most free-spirited plants, which are not always inclined to go by mankind's rules, the speed and extent of spreading will fall within a range. Silver-leaved lamb's ears and artemisias will survive and expand most successfully where soils are sharply drained—light and airy. Where winters are mild, a greater selection of self-sown seeds will survive winter. Seedlings of butterfly bushes, for instance, sprout in abundance in Darell App's New Jersey garden and Edith Eddleman's North Carolina garden but not in my Indiana garden. Where the soil is disturbed or heavily mulched, only the strongest will arise.

A statue catches the eye while colorful plants swirl around it.

Showcasing Free-Spirited Plants

The riots of color within a free-spirited garden are best contained by and contrasted with inset structures or boundaries. Blankets of gold or purple prairie flowers make an attractive scenario, but when silhouetted against a rustic split-rail fence, they become a scene to remember. Strong and highly visible elements such as hedges and walls contain the garden. Walks give it flowing lines and firm up the design. Outdoor benches, stone urns, and statues provide focal points, effective summer and winter, year after year, without needing clipping, fertilizing, or watering.

Other valuable structures, called hardscape, include raised beds, arbors, stone walls or fences, paths, lampposts, clusters of pots, patios, barns, potting sheds, and picnic

Elevating free-spirited plants like this Kamschatka sedum in planters can give them more prominence in the garden.

tables. Natural elements like creeks, rock outcroppings, and picturesque tree trunks are also hardscape.

From a practical perspective, structures add man-made comforts to the outdoors and can help reduce garden maintenance. Paved paths are well suited for walking even when the ground around is wet and spongy. They also can separate two free spirits of an aggressive nature. A raised bed, even a simple square made of landscape timbers, improves growth in shallow, wet, or heavy soils. It also helps keep garden plants in and lawn grass out.

Installing hardscape in a new garden or clearing the way for it in an established garden takes a little extra work and expense. But the effort will reward you for years to come. One way to shortcut hardscape construction is to consider using existing structures around which you might plant a free-spirited garden. A perimeter picket fence, for example, might make a perfect backdrop for rambling cottage-garden plants. When you keep an open mind, great new possibilities might become apparent.

A Gardener's Role

Free-spirited gardening may not be something that you suddenly decide to do one day and then turn the yard upside down to make it happen. It may sneak up on you, one plant at a time. Perhaps a bird drops a seed of a rugosa rose, which becomes a big, beautiful, healthy shrub with fluorescent pink blooms. Or a pink Lenten rose gives birth to a dozen seedlings that grow up to flower in pale cream to deepest rose. Even one free-spirited gift from nature can be enough to make you thirst for more.

Free-spirited gardens may develop when one gardener gives another a plant division, seedling, or envelope of seeds from a favorite free-spirited plant. Easily shared and started in a compatible site, they excite others to try free-spirited gardening and keep alive memories of associated people and places.

You may get your first free-spirited plant at a plant exchange. Like a form of garden currency, clumps of spreaders and self-sown seedlings are swapped for other plants. Tyrant plants, the most aggressive and potentially undesirable of free-spirited species, are usually present in more than modest numbers and should be avoided in most cases.

In my case, free-spirited gardening began when a meadow near my yard sent me plumed offerings—seeds of goldenrods, asters, and milkweeds. One of the most durable and striking free-spirited plants that arrived and prospered is the heath aster (*Aster ericoides*). Growing in neat

*Bearded iris blooms
simultaneously
with oxeye daisies.*

herbaceous bushes to 3 feet high, this aster is totally covered with small white flowers from late summer through fall. While cultivated asters fall prey to diseases, heath asters need nothing but a little sunny space to thrive. Each year, a modest crop of new plants appear, never so many as to be pushy, but plenty to expand the display.

Shirley poppies are another free-spirited flower that came to feel at home in my garden. Curious about a pack of funny-looking seedlings with furry leaves, stems crooked like a shepherd's hook, and tumbledown flower buds, I brought them home from a plant sale. When planted, they straightened up to display glorious clouds of satiny white, pink, and red blooms. The flowers mature to seed capsules, and these dry to sprout pores that, like a pepper shaker, allow the glossy black seeds to sprinkle out. The following spring, two dozen new plants sprang up in unexpected

Shirley poppy flowers, which bloom in white, pink, or red, emerge from crooked buds.

places, and for several years afterward, shirley poppy flowers echoed through the garden.

Unlike traditional gardens, which must regularly be swept clean, free-spirited gardens need weeding primarily when crabgrass, pigweed, or other noxious weeds invade or when seedlings arise in thick bunches. At times you may feel the free-spirited species have spread too far and changed the garden from artistic abandon into chaos. This is when a little judicious editing with hand and hoe help bring the garden back into balance. Tugging larger plants out at the base of the stem when the soil is moist removes them roots and all. In drier weather, sweeping over the soil surface with a hoe uproots smaller seedlings and cuts off the foliage of larger plants.

Perennials such as bee balm that form spreading clumps may need occasional division to rejuvenate their aging center and hold their girth in check. This is best done in spring as the shoots arise or as the plants die back later in the season. Dig up the plant, unearth as much of the root system as possible, and separate it into clumps, teasing the roots apart by hand or using a shovel to cut them apart. Replant the healthiest sections after amending the soil as needed to ensure continued good growth.

Wandering through the garden once a week will show you other ways to encourage free-spirited plants. With the scoop of a trowel, you can move a slightly misplaced seedling to a more suitable spot. A couple snips with pruning shears can eliminate excess seedpods. Colored golf-tee markers can tag plants that are beginning to squeeze out the neighbors and need to be cut back or divided in the future. These kinds of interactions, even the most modest ones, let you subtly mold free-spirited gardens into the image most pleasant to you.

Free-Spirited Gardens in the Landscape

Free-spirited gardens can fill many roles in the yard and need not be relegated to natural landscapes or wilderness gardens. In the coming chapters, you'll see examples of entire gardens filled with free-spirited

Self-seeding forget-me-nots bloom around stationary lenten roses.

23

Seed-Setting Tolerance

Setting seed isn't always pretty, a factor you must consider before planting sweeps of self-seeders. Petals decay or drop and stems and pods brown as the seeds mature, all part of the natural process. Self-seeding cornflowers, shirley poppies, and sunflowers, which can brown out in summer, may prove a distraction for some people. The solution can be to plant early-fading self-seeders in modest numbers or allow only a few to remain in place until they complete their life cycle. Another option is to mingle or replace them with long-blooming annuals, like cockscomb or verbena, that continue to flower even while seeds are developing.

plants and blended gardens combining free spirits with hostas, daylilies, Siberian irises, and other plants not inclined to motility. You will learn ways to use free-spirited annuals, biennials, and perennials in sun or shade, in woodland, prairie, and cutting gardens, amid walks of gravel, and in vegetable and herb gardens.

How you approach free-spirited gardening will depend on the kind of results you want. The most spectacular free-spirited gardens—for instance, the wildflower garden in spring—abound with species that bloom simultaneously. They provide abundant interwoven colors and textures when in flower but fade to quiet foliage the rest of the year.

Curbside in historic New Harmony, Indiana, blue-flowered bearded iris—with broad flowers floating like blue flags—mingle with dancing red and yellow jester caps of wild columbine to provide delicious profusion and contrast. The duo could not be more compatible. Iris spread their thick rhizomes through the bed but leave pockets of soil that can be colonized by self-sown columbine. When the flowers are through, the garden will show a subdued blend of spiky iris leaves and delicately compound columbine leaves to intrigue passersby.

For a simultaneously blooming garden to be successful, all the plants must be vigorous and healthy, a reflection that soil and site are ample for an entire community of compatible plants. One species should not be so vigorous that it smothers the others, which is an oppressive look. To avoid head-on competition, try interweaving deep-rooted and shallow-rooted plants, such as daffodils with forget-me-nots. Or consider sun and shade preferences, allowing sweet alyssum or leaf lettuce, which prefer summer shade, to seed below sun-loving 'Flamingo Feather' cockscomb or cosmos.

Simultaneous flowering—for all its advantages—isn't always the best option for every garden. In small yards or high-profile locations, planning for a succession of color through the growing season may prove more satisfying. Sweeps of spring bloomers—sweet alyssum and calendula—can be replaced by long-blooming self-sowing annuals such as verbena and 'Flamingo Feather' cockscomb.

Gardeners also can plant free-spirited perennials that bloom in succession. But since most perennials bloom only for several weeks to a

Repetition of mauve phlox and golden or orange gloriosa daisies give rhythm to Eve Gardner's cottage garden.

month, more planning will be needed to ensure waves of color progressing through the growing season. It helps to list the times when your favorite perennials bloom, then fill gaps in the bloom calendar with promising free-spirited species you haven't tried before.

Long-lasting color also can come from blending free-spirited plants with reliable, stationary garden plants. Clumps of perennials with limited mobility, like astilbes, peonies, baptisia, Siberian iris, and Russian sage, make ideal companions to clusters of self-sowing annuals and other

A New Look at Lawns

Why begrudge the lawn the quiet blue-green leaves and white-tufted flowers of white clover just because they break up the velvet uniformity of the grass? White clover leaves, handsomely divided, won't brown out in the heat of summer as some lawn grasses do. Charming clover blossoms attract beneficial insects—parasites and predators of pests that help prevent garden problems. Clover roots work in cooperation with nitrogen-fixing bacteria to capture atmospheric nitrogen and convert it to fertilizer, enough to feed the clover and enrich the soil.

Enjoying the advantages of clover requires a readjustment in the prevailing expectations of lawns, a step more homeowners are taking. Motivated by weariness with the cost, trouble, and tediousness of maintaining pristine turf, they may find delight in the forbs that slip into the yard. Fernwood Botanical Garden, in Niles, Michigan, for instance, is a no-spray zone that celebrates when creeping veronica (*Veronica serpyllifolia*) turns the green grass to azure in May. Valerie Strong, in Hudson, Ohio (see page 101), relishes the flowers of dandelions, free-spirited tyrants with brilliant manes of gold. Once the flowers fade, she mows the dandelions back to prevent seed set and spread.

free-spirited plants. Plants with handsome foliage like variegated sages, creeping junipers, and sword-leaved yuccas give form and color to a garden while the free spirits rise and fall around them.

A comforting rhythm develops when colonies of the same free-spirited plants are repeated in the garden, a natural occurrence amid most self-seeders. For garden balance, imagine an invisible line dividing the garden in half. Try to have substantial clusters of the same colors or species on both sides of the division. There is no need for the clusters to be the same size, but the groups should be large enough to be easily visible even from a distance. Another way to encourage balance and rhythm is to edge the garden with a handsome, low creeping plant like deciduous ginger or bugleweed. It will echo the shape of the bed and give it order and dignity.

All gardens, including free-spirited ones, can be more pleasant if some thought is given to coordinating heights. Ground-hugging violets, hidden behind taller bleeding hearts, can't be seen to share their delights. If the violets are set in the foreground of a shaded garden, sweeping their rosettes of heart-shaped leaves and sprightly flowers below uplifted bleeding heart fronds, they can double your pleasure.

Try to organize plants so they build in height toward the rear of a garden viewed from the front or toward the center of a garden viewed from all sides. Of course, they won't stay that way for too long. But by thinning out awkwardly placed self-sown seedlings or rambunctious runners, the general theme can be followed while accommodating some natural ripples and variations.

Color coordination is another option possible in a free-spirited garden. Decide on a color scheme and stick to it, only turning loose plants that are of certain predetermined colors. A quiet garden set close to the house might feature blue and violet flowers with white for contrast. A garden designed for enjoyment on moonlit nights could include predominantly open-faced white or light pastel flowers. A garden that stands proud in the rear of the yard might have sunny yellow and orange flowers. This provides a feeling of organization and control while the free spirits gallop around, peeking up under floral petticoats and whispering in leafy ears.

A self-sown sunflower arises beside a bird feeder of sunflower seeds at Eve Gardner's cottage garden.

Creeping astilbe (ASTILBE CHINENSIS 'PUMILA') drifts in front of a naturalistic grouping of daylilies, persicaria, cannas, purple coneflowers, and purple loosestrife, a notorious spreader.

CHAPTER 2:
wandering perennial gardens

Perennials, plants that live for several to many years, sometimes expand their territory by rising up from creeping stems or wandering roots. Meandering perennials create an impressionistic look, but are open to suggestion and can be turned with a shovel, submerged timber, or wall to take the most artfully pleasing course.

Perennials wander along the road in front of Trudi Temple's wrought iron gate, offering a preview of the garden within.

The larger and more aggressive wandering perennials—plants such as goldenrods, bee balm, and common yarrow—make impressive big stands you can enjoy from afar. In a large yard that needs an equally large garden, they swell into a proportionally pleasing spectacle. The garden quickly becomes full without the gardener having to spend a small fortune on lesser plants.

Bold wanderers are occasionally accused of being weedy, growing in places they aren't wanted. This is almost certain to happen if you try to grow them in small or formally kept gardens. Knowing in advance that they will roam, you can make sure they have sufficient elbow room to spread without bowling over other prized specimens.

Plume poppy, although big and beautiful, can be too aggressive for some gardens.

In smaller gardens or the front of larger gardens, you can color the earth with low-growing, free-spirited ground covers that spread with natural grace around the feet of taller stay-put plants—perennials, shrubs, or trees. Maiden pinks are a good example of a moderate spreader that thrives in sunny spaces with well-drained soil. Friskier creeping jenny can spread a bit faster in moist, fertile soil and may need to be pulled out where it exceeds its welcome.

Low-spreading perennials look great when confined between flagstones. Like a mouse in a maze, they run free through the openings between the stones but always find in the end that they are captive. Mat formers such as moss phlox, maiden pinks, and snow-in-summer might also spread out to sun themselves on top of the rocks, giving a stone walk or patio a cottage-garden ambience.

One of the most important qualities of wandering perennials is their foliage, which is on display in large swaths. 'Burgundy Glow' bugle-weed—with oval leaves shimmering pink, white, and green and short spikes of blue flowers—might bump up against narrow blue-green leaves of creeping maiden pinks, an interesting contrast in foliage texture. But another surprise is in store when the maiden pinks open rosy wall-to-wall flowers that reflect pink highlights in the bugleweed foliage.

Nearby several clusters of silver-leaved snow-in-summer might cascade over edging rocks and flash white flowers to the sun, their brightness connecting with the creamy colors of the bugleweed leaves. Although early summer has only just begun, these tapestries of handsome foliage and their supporting flowers have already set the tone for the season.

Deeper in the garden, where plants grow taller, a summer ocean of bee balm spreads in luxury, showing off shaggy heads of aromatic red flowers that appeal to hummingbirds and butterflies. Bee balm foliage starts the season looking neat and smelling of a perfumed mint. Later in the summer, it is likely to become disfigured with powdery mildew. If the bright flowers and wonderful fragrance incline you to use it anyway, you can wait until disease strikes, cut the stems off, and let the plant resprout

Above, stone steps make an ideal stage for creeping plants. Left, Moss phlox spreads over a low retaining wall to the rocks below.

fresh. As fall nears, pink flower spikes of obedient plants lap around the perimeter of boltonia, an upright noncreeper covered with a blizzard of small white flowers. This is a garden that will see the season out with a flamboyant style all its own.

Certain creepers, such as goutweed (*Aegopodium podagraria*), chameleon plant (*Houttuynia cordata*), lily of the valley (*Convallaria majalis*), yellow loosestrife (*Lysimachia punctata*), purple-leaf loosestrife (*Lysimachia ciliata* 'Purpurea'), and gooseneck loosestrife (*Lysimachia clethroides*) have been excluded from this chapter because the chances of them becoming invasive run high. Some of these tyrants have long memories and come back to haunt your garden from deep, persistent roots or small pieces of stem left behind in the soil.

Trudi Temple enjoys rearranging the perennials in her garden.

Creepers Between a Rock and a Hard Place

Trudi Temple, raised in the rich heritage of a German gardening family, exercises her green thumb in a one-acre suburban yard in Hinsdale, Illinois. She likes large bold plants and rich combinations of foliage textures and colors. Preferring to know where plants will arise, she has eliminated most self-seeders, with a few irresistible exceptions like purple coneflowers and fragrant white-flowered *Nicotiana sylvestris*. But she has opened the door wide for some of the best free-spirited creeping plants.

Spotlighted like stars on the stage, creeping perennials are bunched in irregular openings between huge stone slab steps, a placid background for dynamic foliage. A stairway in light shade features elongated silver-mottled foliage of lungwort, which spreads on underground stems, elbow to elbow with bergenia and its rounded clusters of lettuce-like leaves, which arise over slowly creeping roots. In sharp contrast, a golden ribbon of creeping jenny (*Lysimachia nummularia* 'Aurea') angles through narrower spaces, its creeping stems hugging the angles of the rock.

The micro-drama is much different between the sun-drenched rocks at the entryway steps. Fine-leaved and fragrant thyme blends into

Red-flowered bee
balm echoes the
color of 'Velvet Star'
daylily at Trudi
Temple's garden.

bugleweed. The openings terminate in the succulent rosettes of hen-and-chicks, with agave-shaped mother rosettes surrounded by their smaller offspring, still connected by umbilical cords of fleshy stems.

Edgings are another place where creepers are likely to be found. White bloody cranesbill (*Geranium sanguineum* 'Alba'), a wide-spreading and leisurely creeping perennial with deeply cut leaves and open-faced white flowers, stands at the feet of clusters of daylilies and coneflowers.

Front and center in a shady part of the garden is a rhizoma-tous astilbe (*Astilbe chinensis* 'Pumila'), sweeping along a stone edging and casting feathered purple flower plumes in front of large-leaved hostas, daylilies, and fountain grasses. Deeper in the shade, slowly

Above, hybrid yarrow flowers mingle with spikes of lamb's ears. Left, tawny daylilies mark the entryway to a German Village vegetable garden.

creeping European ginger, foamflowers, and epimedium mingle amid hostas, merry-bells, and trilliums.

In the back of one border, plume poppies, with huge lobed leaves and upright feathery flowers, make a handsome backdrop for a birdbath. Elsewhere red bee balm struts beside 'Velvet Star' daylily and red-leaf amaranth.

Creeping perennials must prove their merit before being welcomed into Temple's gardens, a philosophy that may work well for you. New perennials are evaluated in a separate trial garden to see how they will perform. If they grow well and are not too aggressive, they will be divided and transplanted in one or several places. Any perennials that become bullies when on trial may never reach the main gardens.

Daylilies and Their Creeping Companions

One of the stalwart foundations of the flower garden is the daylily, beautiful, durable, and reliable. Its open trumpet-shaped flowers now come in every color but blue. Flower buds cluster on special flowering stems, each bud opening into a flower for just one day on a rhythm so regular you could set your clock by it. The straplike foliage arches upward from the ground, filling the garden without making a spectacle. Because they grow in sun or shade and heavy or lean soils, there are daylilies that are ideal for any garden.

The old-fashioned, orange-flowered tawny daylily *(Hemerocallis fulva* 'Europa') is a mover and shaker that spreads on rhizomes. A native of Asia, it has crept through Europe and the United States and glows in the ditches beside country roads in summer. In the German Village area of Columbus, Ohio, orange daylilies light up the entire town in early summer, having swept in front of stores, beside parking lots, and across tree lawns.

Modern daylilies, however, have had the run bred out of them while having more colors, shapes, and forms bred into them. They are primarily clump formers, expanding gradually and slowly. Gardens rich in these new daylilies can benefit from some creeping companions to fill in around them. Darell Apps, daylily breeder from New Jersey, enjoys using silver foliage as a backdrop for daylilies and other perennials. For many years, this job was taken by a modestly creeping form of 'Silver King' artemisia (*Artemisia ludoviciana* var. *albula* 'Silver King'), a California native that makes silver-leaved thickets 3 feet tall. New forms he has tried lately have proven more aggressive and less desirable and may be best grown where root barriers will prevent excessive spread.

For the garden foreground, Apps likes the silver and gold chrysanthemum (*Chrysanthemum pacificum*), which has silver-edged leaves that spread like a tide across well-drained soil. Where frost arrives late in fall, it will produce small golden flowers as the growing season ebbs. While thriving in the mild New Jersey winters, it is not reliably hardy in many colder northern climates.

Persicaria, purple loosestrife, astilbes, daylilies and alliums along Trudi Temple's front garden fence.

Horticultural Hints

Some free-spirited creepers move in a modest fashion, colonizing new areas without smothering neighboring plants. But when growing conditions are ideal, even an ordinarily modest mover may kick up its heels and go looking for more new turf. Larger wandering perennials tend to move in a big way and may quickly achieve billowing abundance. Sometimes planting in a little shade or near the roots of trees and shrubs will naturally put a damper on overexuberant growth. If not, you can cut wandering perennials back with pruning shears or mowers, or dig up ill-placed clumps and turn them loose in a garden where they can be truly wild and spread unhindered.

Minimizing manhandling requires a little advance preparation. Limit spread with physical barriers such as submerged timbers, cement walks and foundations, or large, plastic nursery pots and big clay drain tiles. Slow down creeping stems by leaving the rim of a spread-stopping container an inch or two above the soil surface. The lawn makes a good boundary for taller growers that are kept in check by regular mowing, but can be permeated by bugleweed and other low creepers.

38

When growing wandering plants, division will become part of your garden vocabulary. As perennials creep beyond their artistic boundaries or begin to age and fade out in the center, division is the solution. Dig up the plant, keeping as many roots as possible intact, and use a shovel or knife to separate off healthy young sections to replant. You can distribute extra divisions through the garden, giving it the rhythm of repeated color. Or simply replant one section, reshaping the garden to resemble an earlier time, two, three, or five years ago, when the perennial was small.

Potted Wanderers, Subdued Garden Reflections

An elegant way to give a garden of wandering perennials form and focus is to set large pots and planters of the same wandering perennials in the corners or in other strategic places near the front of the garden. Pots also can go on nearby patios and decks. The captive wandering perennials repeat foliage and flowers within the surrounding garden, giving the entire space rhythm. Because the pots stand out amid the greenery, use nice-looking ones such as good-quality terra-cotta containers, ceramic pots with drainage holes in the bottom, or plastics molded into decorative shapes or terra-cotta look-alikes.

From a practical perspective, some of the best perennials to use in pots are drought-tolerant maiden pinks, snow-in-summer, evening primrose, and creeping sedums. When interplanted, they form an interesting combination of foliage and succession of flowers. Plants like bee balm, hardy ageratum, and obedient plants, which insist on moist soil, can be grown solo in large pots equipped with bottom moisture reservoirs to keep them going when you can't be there to water them.

*Bee balm mingles
with pansies in
Valerie Strong's
garden.*

Glossary of Wandering Perennials

Some of the most impressive creeping and spreading perennials are listed here. Slowly expanding clump formers, which do not in my mind qualify as free-spirited, have been omitted. You'll find additional spreading free-spirited perennials in other chapters of this book and can use them similarly to the following plants.

'Summer Pastels', a hybrid of common yarrow, create large drifts of soft-colored flowers.

COMMON YARROW
(Achillea millefolium)

Hardiness: Zones 3 to 9
Exposure: Sun
Some Companions: Ornamental grasses, coneflowers, Frikart's aster, spiderwort, 'Silver King' artemisia
Primary Means of Spreading: Creeping stems and seeds
Aggressiveness: Moderate to aggressive
Flowering Time: Summer

Delicate feathery leaves grow in low mats, expanding in diameter as much as several feet per year as underground stems surface and sprout ferny rosettes. Flowering stems rise 1½ to 3 feet high and bear graceful flat-topped white, pink, or red flower clusters, wonderful for flower arrangements. Once the terminal flowers fade, you can cut back stems to round plump flower-bud clusters lower on the stem for additional bloom. As the flowers fade, the heads turn brown and bear abundant seeds. Where winters are mild, common yarrow leaves can remain evergreen. Although a native of Eurasia, common yarrow is widely naturalized in the United States, fooling some people into believing it is a native wildflower. The aromatic leaves, once believed to be love charms, also have been used as medicines for treating nosebleeds and headaches.

Provide well-drained soil on the lean side to discourage flopping stems and rampant spreading. Divide every couple years for renewal and size control.

BUGLEWEED
(Ajuga reptans)

Hardiness: Zones 3 to 9
Exposure: Sun to light shade
Some Companions: Japanese anemone, columbines, baptisias, bellflowers
Primary Means of Spreading: Creeping stems
Aggressiveness: Moderate to aggressive
Flowering Time: Spring

Whorled clusters of spoon-shaped leaves form ground-covering mats of green, bronze, variegated, or tricolor foliage linked by creeping stems. Most varieties of bugleweed stay compact—about 4 inches tall—but 'Catlin's Giant', with extra-large bronze-tinted foliage, can reach 10 inches. Common ajuga has small spikes of blue flowers in spring, but certain cultivars sport white or pink flowers instead. Bugleweed, which is of European origin, is often used as an edging or ground cover and may be seen lingering in abandoned gardens long after other plants are gone. It can spread quickly, growing beneath, around, or through neighboring plants and even out into the grass.

Bugleweed adapts to many soils but does best in moist well-drained soil of reasonable fertility. Cut back old flower spikes when done blooming to keep plants tidy and prevent self-seeding and production of off-type seedlings.

PURPLE ROCKCRESS
(Aubrieta deltoidea)

Hardiness: Zones 4 to 8
Exposure: Sun
Some Companions: Snow-in-summer, hardy alyssum, late spring bulbs
Primary Means of Spreading: Creeping stems and seeds
Aggressiveness: Moderate
Flowering Time: Summer

Spring comes to life when this perennial erupts with purple, blue, or red flowers. A carpet of small grayish leaves creeps close to the ground, remaining under 6 inches high. It looks nice spreading between flagstones or over a retaining wall, and draping from an opening in an old stone wall. The four-petaled flowers open in clusters over the top of the leaves, then mature into elongated, bristly seedpods.

An alpine plant originating in the mountians of Sicily, Greece, and Asia Minor, purple rockcress grows best in sharply drained soil. Cut old flowering stems back by half or more when done blooming to tidy up the foliage for the remainder of the growing season. You can leave a few stems to produce seed if self-seeding is desired.

Clustered Bellflower
(Campanula glomerata)

Hardiness: Zones 3 to 9
Exposure: Sun to light shade
Some Companions: Lady's mantle, Siberian iris, meadow-sweet, bee balm, columbines
Primary Means of Spreading: Creeping stems
Aggressiveness: Moderate
Flowering Time: Summer

With bold clusters of bell-shaped, cool violet or white flowers on stems that can reach 3 feet tall, this is a majestic plant if allowed to spread. It may form an open ground cover, leaving openings for self-seeders like columbine to intermingle. The oval leaves may be slightly scalloped. Clustered bellflowers, natives of Eurasia, may persist for years in vintage gardens on older properties.

Provide moist soil, water during dry weather, and cut back the first crop of flowers to encourage more bloom. Divide as needed for rejuvenation. If you like clustered bellflower, look into some other free-spirited species such as *Campanula garganica* and *C. poscharskyana*.

Both the silver foliage and the white flowers of Snow-in-Summer seem to glow with reflected light.

Snow-in-Summer
(Cerastium tomentosum)

Hardiness: Zones 2 to 7
Exposure: Sun
Some Companions: Yarrow, armeria, thyme, pinks, roses
Primary Means of Spreading: Creeping stems and seeds
Aggressiveness: Moderate to aggressive
Flowering Time: Late spring and early summer

If there was one plant that exemplified a free-spirited spreader, this would be it. Distinctive and striking when growing at the edge of a raised bed or bordering a walk, snow-in-summer spreads a silver carpet of lance-shaped leaves to cascade down and dangle their toes on the pavement. They are particularly charming when covered with a blizzard of white flowers in late spring.

Native to the mountains of Italy, this plant does best in cool climates. Provide sharply drained soil and plenty of sun. In hot, humid climates, free air circulation may prevent disease . Cut stems halfway back after blooming and divide as needed.

Plumbago
(Ceratostigma plumbaginoides)

Hardiness: Zones 5 to 9
Exposure: Sun to partial shade
Some Companions: Peonies, asters, boltonia, coreopsis, sedums
Primary Means of Spreading: Creeping stems
Aggressiveness: Moderate
Flowering Time: Summer and fall

Plumbago forms a subdued mantle of low-growing oval leaves that can spread on pencil-thick rhizomes beneath shrubs and trees or across the front of a flower border. While the base of older plants may become woody, the stems are herbaceous and die back every year. New growth emerges late in spring, when you're just about to give up hope. In late summer and fall, plumbago erupts with cheerful blue flowers—just when all the other flowers are turning golden and bronze. In fall, the leaves change to burgundy, complementing other autumn leaves. A native of western China, plumbago is a little like a new kid on the block in many American gardens.

Well-drained but moist and fertile soil is ideal. Divide as needed for multiplication and control.

Green-and-Gold
(Chrysogonium virginiatum)

Hardiness: Zones 5 to 9
Exposure: Sun to light shade
Some Companions: Daylilies, hostas, woodland wildflowers
Primary Means of Spreading: Creeping stems and seeds
Aggressiveness: Moderate
Flowering Time: Spring, occasionally summer and fall

43

This wildflower, native to the eastern United States, makes a charming ground cover beneath deciduous shrubs and trees, along the borders of paths, and at the edges of garden beds. Rosettes of hairy oval leaves spread side by side on brittle rhizomes, slowly but steadily expanding colony size. The arrival of golden daisylike flowers—distinctive with five outer florets around a sterile central disk—begins early in spring, peaking in mid to late spring, and continuing in scattered bursts in summer and fall. Each flower may produce up to five little nutlets, not a large seed crop. With the long flowering season, however, and the easygoing nature of this plant, plenty of self-sown seedlings are bound to arise. Green-and-gold foliage can stay green deep into winter, particularly in mild climates.

Provide well-drained, rich organic soil for best results. Occasional division may be necessary to renew plants.

MAIDEN PINKS
(Dianthus deltoides)

Hardiness: Zones 3 to 9
Exposure: Sun
Some Companions: Hardy geraniums, creeping baby's breath, 'Palace Purple' coralbells, catmint, evening primrose
Primary Means of Spreading: Creeping stems and seeds
Aggressiveness: Limited to moderate
Flowering Time: Summer

These charming, fragrant cottage garden plants from Europe were once believed to represent true love, and were given by hopeful suitors to lovely ladies. Rhizomes sprout offshoots while stems creep along the ground to consume more space. In summer the entire plant is covered with multitudes of fragrant single pink, white, or red flowers, often fringed and centered with a red eye. The flowers can reach 1 foot

high, the flowering stems easily cut back with grass shears when the blooms fade. If old flowers are left untouched, they can produce capsules swollen with abundant seeds and the possibilities of self-sown seedlings. Maiden pinks can spread in the front of a garden bed, beside retaining walls, and amid stones in a walk, where they will creep artistically over soil and stone alike.

Well-drained soil helps ensure good winter survival. Deadhead to extend bloom period and divide every couple years to prolong lifetime.

CREEPING JENNY OR MONEYWORT
(Lysimachia nummularia)

Hardiness: Zones 3 to 8
Exposure: Sun to light shade
Some Companions: Daylilies, heliopsis, coneflowers
Primary Means of Spreading: Creeping stems
Aggressiveness: Moderate to aggressive
Flowering Time: Late spring to early summer

Shiny leaves so round they resemble coins are borne on fast-creeping stems that root as they go. 'Aurea' is a golden-leaved form that blends particularly well with golden-variegated or golden-flowered plants. Star-shaped yellow flowers open over the foliage, making a lively show.

A member of a particularly aggressive genus, this low grower is related to garden bullies like gooseneck loosestrife (*Lysimachia clethroides*), fringed loosestrife (*L. ciliata*), and yellow loosestrife (*L. punctata*), which are difficult to eliminate from a garden once inadvertently planted. Like its kin, creeping jenny is

occasionally accused of invasiveness, particularly in moist, fertile soils that encourage its rapid spread. Although European, creeping jenny has spread throughout much of the eastern United States. When limited to a garden setting, it is easily handled by pulling up overgrown sections, held in place only by shallow roots.

BEE BALM
(Monarda didyma)

Hardiness: Zones 4 to 8
Exposure: Sun to light shade
Some Companions: Hardy geraniums, bellflowers, daylilies, shasta daisies
Primary Means of Spreading: Creeping stems
Aggressiveness: Aggressive
Flowering Time: Summer

Shaggy red, pink, purple, or white flowers stand about 3 feet high atop spicily scented foliage used to flavor Earl Gray tea or to make herb tea. The flowers of this American native from the East and Midwest are a haven for bees, butterflies, and hummingbirds. Creeping stems spread into irregular drifts, arising around and amid other plants and moving particularly fast in light, loose, and fertile soil.

This native of wet stream banks and moist meadows grows best in moist, rich soil. Plan to water during drought. Mulching with compost instead of fertilizing encourages good growth without excessive spread. If bee balm needs to be kept away from neighboring plants, frequent division may be necessary. Powdery mildew may disfigure leaves but can be overcome by cutting plants back to the ground so they can resprout healthy new growth. New cultivars with some resistance are now available.

PINK EVENING PRIMROSE

(Oenothera speciosa)

Hardiness: Zones 5 to 8
Exposure: Sun
Some Companions: Hardy geraniums, Siberian iris, balloon flower, bellflowers
Primary Means of Spreading: Creeping stems
Aggressiveness: Aggressive
Flowering Time: Summer

Large open-faced pink flowers stand atop plants 1 to 2 feet tall. While some other evening primroses bloom in the evening, these flowers open during the day to give a sparkling show. Especially long blooming, they are charmers that spread boldly into ground covers. The rhizomes responsible can sometimes be invasive and should be used only where there is plenty of open property to colonize. The unassuming elongated or oval leaves sometimes are lobed.

Native from Kansas to Texas, pink evening primroses require well-drained soil and can be drought tolerant once well established. Divide as often as needed for creep control.

OBEDIENT PLANT

(Physostegia virginiana)

Hardiness: Zones 3 to 9
Exposure: Sun to light shade
Some Companions: Chrysanthemums, asters, boltonia, ornamental grasses
Primary Means of Spreading: Creeping stems
Aggressiveness: Moderate to aggressive
Flowering Time: Late summer and fall

A native across much of the eastern United States, obedient plant has four-rowed

Spikes of bright obedient plant flowers liven up any garden late in the growing season.

spikes of pale to hot pink or white flowers standing atop 2- to 4-foot-tall stems of elongated leaves. With a finger, you can turn the flowers on the stem so they will all face one way or another, which may be why these plants are called obedient. They are far from obedient when it comes to spreading and can move quickly on creeping underground stems without even asking, "May I?" This can result in charming, bold drifts of color in the middle or rear of a large perennial garden or even in a meadow garden.

For best growth and spread, provide moist garden soil. In especially fertile soil, obedient plants may be prone to flopping. Compact cultivars like 'Vivid' are more likely to be self-supporting. Divide as desired to control colony size.

KAMTSCHATICUM CREEPING SEDUM

(Sedum kamtschaticum)

Hardiness: Zones 3 to 8
Exposure: Sun
Some Companions: Creeping thyme, wooly thyme, maiden pinks, showy sedum, daylilies
Primary Means of Spreading: Creeping stems
Aggressiveness: Moderate to aggressive
Flowering Time: Spring and summer

Many creeping sedums have interesting foliage and abundant, though small, flowers and make charming free-spirited ground covers for sun. Prostrate stems emerge from a mother plant, spreading across open earth and beneath nearby plants, then breaking out with clusters of foliage and flowers. The creeping stems continue in this fashion to cover a considerable amount of turf. Kamtschaticum sedum, a native of eastern Asia, sprouts short upright stems from its runners. They are clad with narrow leaves, clusters of starry golden orange flowers, and later red fruit. An even more colorful variegated form has white-edged leaves.

Provide creeping sedums with average to lean soil with good drainage. Occasional division may be necessary. Several related creeping sedums also are worth exploring. White stonecrop (*Sedum album*) has narrow evergreen leaves and white flowers. Two-row sedum (*S. spurium*) has pink flowers and rosettes of rounded leaves, some blushed with burgundy, or white and pink.

45

CHAPTER 3:
come-as-you-may cut flowers

One of the most wonderful ways to get up close and personal with your garden is by cutting the flowers and bringing them indoors to anywhere you linger longest—kitchen, bedroom, or home office. The best flowers to cut for this purpose are long-stemmed beauties, able to hold their heads high when arranged in a vase.

While ordinary florist roses and carnations grow in utilitarian rows in working gardens, the free-spirited garden yields a unique blend of unusual cut flowers that spread with self-sown seeds. They dance around the bed from year to year, sometimes arising in beautiful and novel combinations well worth remembering for future arrangements and garden plans.

Self-sowing muskmallows (MALVA MOSCHATA), foxglove, and verbascums mingle with golden thyme.

For a lighthearted start on this project, consider planting annual larkspurs, with feathery leaves and stately, upright spires of majestic white, blue, and pink flowers, or biennial foxglove, a harmonious companion with spikes of tubular purple flowers. Later in the season, flowering tobacco billows with vivacious trumpet-shaped red or pink flowers, beautifully interspersed with stiffer upright plumes of silver and soft pink 'Flamingo Feather' celosia. A garden rich with these free-spirited flowers will be draped in a veil of color.

A self-seeding cut flower garden needs firm and fast boundaries within which the flowers can play an action-packed annual game of musical chairs. Containing the garden within a simple rectangular raised bed gives it needed structure, while providing space to improve the soil and speed the rate of water drainage.

A framework of stationary cut flowers, such as clusters of arcing, sunny yellow daylilies, pink-blushed and prickly-stemmed roses, milky white peonies thick and heavy with flower petals, and late-arriving chrysanthemums, infuses comforting stability into a free-spirited cut flower garden. Rhythmically repeated clusters of annual cut flowers, such as long-limbed, powder blue ageratums and sun-dazzled extra-tall zinnias, are easily added to any sunny garden for structure and, of course, for bouquets. Where long-awaited color is slow to arrive in spring, blend in rainbow-flowered tulips, slowly drifting daffodils, and other early-rising bulbs.

Such leisurely gardens of free-spirited cut flowers can be a source of delight—indoors and out—through most of the growing season.

Unusual Cuts in Don Vanderbrook's Garden

When behind the scenes at a party, Don Vanderbrook, internationally known floral designer, creates magical gardenesque settings with trees, shrubs, bamboo, topiaries, and boatloads of flowers. Vanderbrook has decorated such places as the White House and the British Embassy in Washington, D.C., and the Fairmont Hotel in San Francisco. But no matter where he is, Vanderbrook gleans ideas from his country garden outside Cleveland, Ohio.

Vanderbrook's gentle backyard hillside is divided with long,

49

rectangular raised beds to make a series of terraces filled with flowers for cutting. The beds are separated by brick walks or mulched paths, trellised espaliers, and low hedges of boxwood. A central allée runs along an aged brick walk and past a graceful figurine in the center of the garden to a meadow of flowering trees on the hillside beyond.

The effect is of a formal series of garden rooms brimming with prolific assortments of self-sowing plants. An original color scheme of pink and blue on one side and orange and yellow on the other has blended as seedlings have found their way into neighboring gardens, a blurring Vanderbrook finds pleasing. Seedlings arise and thrive where

conditions are right, often performing better than when planted.

One of the places Vanderbrook commonly finds self-sown seedlings is in the walks between garden beds. Mulched paths, replenished each spring with wood chips, slowly break down into rich organic material during the ensuing year. By early spring, they have become a moist, fertile medium for seedlings, which arise just in time to be moved into proper growing spaces before the walk is remulched. Brick walks are quick to warm up in the spring sun and stay moist with frequent April showers. The combination seems to bring out the best in seeds, which sprout in dense thickets that make Vanderbrook wonder if he shouldn't start all his seeds between bricks.

Vanderbrook seeks out novel flowers to enjoy in his yard, collecting some as seeds from promising-looking roadside wildflowers such as a white-flowered bouncing bet (*Saponaria officinalis*) from Vermont and a white-flowered meadow rue growing beside the Pennsylvania Turnpike. He imports other seeds from England, Germany, and the Netherlands.

Elegant foxglove flowers border a garden path.

Foxgloves of many species have a prominent place in the garden. Vanderbrook raves about little-known foxglove species with flowers of green, white, yellow, and brown, which he imports from England. He also finds interesting volunteer seedlings of common foxgloves (*Digitalis purpurea*), elegant plants with graceful, one-sided spikes of lilac-purple flowers with a light-spotted throat. Self-sown flowers occasionally tip their ordinarily nodding, trumpetlike chins upward to show off the flashy throat. Several others bear flowers all around the stem, a big improvement over the ordinary one-sided spikes. These plants are tagged and allowed to go to seed to see if the offspring will be as enticing as the mother plant.

'Russell Hybrid' lupines have gone through several generations in the garden and changed from brilliant colors to a subdued companionable blend of pink, mauve, and purple. To use them for cutting, Vanderbrook wraps newly cut lupine flower spikes in a sheath of newspaper and immediately puts them in a bucket of water for a couple hours. This keeps the flower spikes upright while they drink up the water, grow firmer, and get ready to hold their own in an arrangement.

CAMPANULA PUNCTATA *mingles with volunteer lupines.*

51

Some of the charming and less common bellflowers are included in this garden. Among them is Asian *Campanula punctata*, which has clusters of large, drooping, broad-sided bells that are white to pink or maroon. Both a creeper and a self-seeder, it has a way of moving quietly but efficiently. In summer, biennial nettle-leaved bellflower (*C. trachelium*), a Eurasian native, drips with nodding bells of blue, purple, or white. This species naturalizes and grows like wild in parts of the United States.

When cut from the garden and put on center stage in a flower arrangement, these and many other free-spirited flowers make handsome displays and inspire conversation.

A Worldwide Phenomenon: the Peony-Flowered Poppy

The peony-flowered (opium) poppy (*Papaver somniferum*) grows well from coast to coast, a remarkable testimony to its adaptability. It spreads across a cabbage garden in Anchorage, Alaska, covering the somber blue-green cabbage heads with a rainbow of bright open-faced flowers. At Gardenview Botanical Garden in Strongsville, Ohio, it fills a June garden with cheerful color, then fades to allow self-sown *Verbena bonariensis* and spider flowers (*Cleome hassleriana*) to take over for the rest of the season. In San Diego, California, it frolics through Judy Wigand's subtropical garden. Wigand selects bright pink- and red-flowered types to go to seed and thus coaxes new generations into her favorite color range. Gertrude Jeckyll, nineteenth-century British garden designer, blended it into the flower borders at Munstead. Englishman Christopher Lloyd lets it self-seed in his famous garden at Great Dixter.

Originally a native of Turkey, Persia, India, and China, this poppy has been grown for the harvest of opium, which is illegal in the United States. Instead, it's grown here for its flowers, which are great for cutting.

Wild *P. somniferum* have a pale lilac flower with a central purple spot and a fluffy ring of stamens. Modern cultivated varieties range from single- to double-flowered forms in pink, red, purple, and white. Growing on 3- to 4-foot-high stems, flowers can reach to 5 inches across. Each flower doesn't last long, but if you remove the fading blooms, new blossoms can continue to appear lower on the stem. Instead of deadheading, you can let the

Peony-flowered poppies billow beside a narrow walk.

52

flowers mature into pale, waxy-looking seed heads, also nice for arrangements. For particularly unusual seedpods, look for 'Hen and Chickens', with a large mother pod surrounded by little pods.

Once the seedpods begin to dry, the tiny kidney-shaped seeds are mature and ready to be set free in the garden. You can break the pods open and shake the seeds around or let some escape naturally as you cut off the old stems and seedpods and carry them out of the garden. For best growth, provide rich, moist soil and full sun.

Texas bluebonnets contrast dramatically with a yellow-blossomed wildflower at the National Wildflower Research Center in Austin, Texas.

Like other poppies, *P. somniferum* contains a milky sap that can leak out when cut, causing the stem to wilt. Immediately after cutting, Don Vanderbrook dips the cut stem ends in boiling water for eighteen seconds to seal them closed before using them in an arrangement.

Texas Bluebonnets, Southwestern Specialties

The Texas bluebonnet (*Lupinus texensis*) is a wildflower that has captured America's imagination. Thousands of spikes of crystal blue pea-shaped flowers spread across Austin-area fields and roadsides in late spring, drawing tourists, photographers, and artists from around the country for the spectacle. While the wild bluebonnets should be left undisturbed to procreate, garden-grown Texas bluebonnets make charming cut flowers.

Growing in the alkaline rocky soils of the droughty Texas hill country, bluebonnets are annual legumes that arise in fall or early spring and bloom in March and April. They thrive with a little help from nitrogen-fixing bacteria, symbiotes that live on legume roots, capture atmospheric nitrogen, and convert it to fertilizer. First-time growers can purchase preinnoculated seed for nitrogen-fixing benefits.

Fall is a mild, moist season in Texas, ideal for planting bluebonnet seeds. The new seedlings stay low through the mild winter, then grow steadily during the warm, moist weather of early spring. To encourage a fast break when first planting bluebonnets, rub the seeds between two pieces of sandpaper to help wear down the thick and armored seed coat. Since self-sown seeds are in nature's hands, expect it to take several years for rain and soil grit to thin the seed coat enough to allow germination.

Multiplying Bulbs

Many bulbs have potential for use in a free-spirited cut flower garden. Some spread by begetting new bulbs or corms, clones that become mirror-image look-alikes. With daffodils, for instance, a single bulb will produce a new bulblet each year, slowing expanding into a clump.

Wild hyacinth (*Triteleia hyacintha* syn. *Brodiaea lactea*), a west coast native, spreads in a more free-spirited manner on rapidly multiplying corms that transform into colonies of low, grasslike leaves. In summer, they produce superb cut flowers, upward-facing bell-shaped blooms of white, blue, or lavender on $2\frac{1}{2}$-foot-long stems. Wild hyacinth has a surprisingly broad hardiness range that spans across much of the United States in protected sites from northern Ohio to Georgia and southern California. All it asks is well-drained soil and plenty of sun.

In the nearly tropical warmth of San Diego, expansion rates can accelerate even more. Free-spirited spreaders such as freesias, South African natives with vivid flowers of red, orange, yellow, purple, or lavender blue; 'Paper White' narcissus with clusters of fragrant white daffodil-like flowers; and alstroemerias with tall, elegant, red, orange, white, or yellow flowers multiply rambunctiously for Judy Wigand.

Other bulbs have more far-reaching strategies, spreading by seed to colonize wider areas. In cool climates, self-seeders are limited primarily to smaller bulbs like Siberian squill and snowdrops, good for use in small bud vases.

In warm climates, a few larger, long-stemmed bulbs can grow quickly into flowering plants from seed. In Edith Eddleman's North

Carolina garden, for example, the Formosa lily (*Lilium formosanum*) grows from a February-sown seedling into a blooming bulb by fall. Huge, fragrant white flowers can stretch to 8 feet high on mature bulbs. When the flowers fade, the upright-facing seedpods are splendid to cut for dried flower arrangements. But shake the seeds out first so you can have a new crop of bulbs in the works. Tolerating intense heat in southern climates, Formosa lilies also are winter hardy to about -15° F.

Rustic fencing and trellises give Don Vanderbrook's free-spirited cutting garden visual strength.

Horticultural Hints

With a little careful management, a free-spirited cut flower garden can replenish itself and provide a heart-warming variety of interesting flowers for a vase. The secret is to let some of the flowers go to seed, instead of capturing them all for flower arrangements. Preserving those with the most beautiful flowers, however difficult, will encourage a new population that may share or even better their parents' performance.

Consider how the seeds are strewn. Some plants have lightweight seeds that can move some distance across the garden. Among the best examples of this are the parachute-clad seeds of milkweeds and butterfly weeds, whose fluffy plumes can float on breezes to alight on the other side of the garden. The smaller seeds of plants such as larkspur, shirley poppies, and peony-flowered poppies can scatter. Others such as muskmallow (*Abelmoschus moschatus*), sweet peas, and cannas have heavier seeds that drop underneath the skirts of the parent to form fairly tight-knit clusters.

To encourage self-seeding, leave open soil for the seeds to settle in and keep the area undisturbed until they arise. Marking a seedling nursery with a colored tag or golf tee will help remind you that this is a no-trespass area.

Raised Beds and Accessories

Following Don Vanderbrook's lead, consider using a rectangular raised bed for the cut flower garden. It can fit conveniently into the sunny perimeters of the yard or can be nestled close to the south side of the house, within reach when you need a bouquet for the kitchen table.

The most easily tended raised beds are not more than 4 feet wide, allowing you to reach into the center without stepping on the garden soil. Using landscape timbers, create an edging 3 to 6 inches high, making sure all the timbers are level and soundly secured to the ground. Build a deep base of loose soil within the bed, adding extra organic matter to improve the texture of lean or heavy soil. If you have room for two beds, you can separate them with a gravel or mulch path or patio, which adds impact to the design and allows for easy access in wet weather.

For even more structure and charm, you can back a free-spirited cut flower garden with a lath trellis, ideal for lightweight flowering vines like sweet peas and morning glories. At the simplest, install two upright timbers at each end of the bed and stretch nylon mesh between them. For a more elaborate trellis, lash together diagonal sapling branches or bamboo stakes to make crossing supports and an open diamond pattern.

A series of rectangular
raised beds is cut into
Don Vanderbrook's gentle
hillside.

Glossary of Free-Spirited Cut Flowers

Chosen primarily for their interesting colors, shapes, and textures, these free-spirited cut flowers run the gamut from annuals and biennials (plants that produce foliage the first year and finish their lives with flowers and seeds the second year) to perennials. Consult hardiness, exposure, and soil specifics to determine how these plants will self-sow for you. In colder climates or where the soil is disturbed or mulched, there is likely to be less self-sowing.

'FLAMINGO FEATHER' COCKSCOMB

(Celosia spicata syn. C. argentea Spicata group)

Hardiness: Annual
Exposure: Sun
Some Companions: Dame's rocket, oxeye daisy, sweet alyssum, verbena
Primary Means of Spreading: Seeds
Aggressiveness: Limited to moderate
Flowering Time: Summer and fall

This old-fashioned annual of tropical origin, also called wheat celosia, has returned to popularity in recent years. It has soft pink, upright flower spikes that elongate through the summer, sprouting new pink flowers at the top and aging to silver at the bottom. Because the flowers remain attractive all season, you can leave them standing in the garden in summer, fall, and even winter. This provides an extended opportunity to release the abundant, small dark seeds, some of which are likely to grow into volunteer seedlings. The flowers last equally long when cut and put in a vase but are best used when young so they won't shed seeds indoors. The plants can grow 1 to 4 feet high, neatly attired in simple, oval to elongated, point-tipped leaves.

Provide fertile, moist soil, watering during dry weather.

'Blue Cloud' larkspur contrasts with orange nasturtiums.

FIELD LARKSPUR

(Consolida ambigua syn. Delphinium ajacis)

Hardiness: Annual
Exposure: Sun
Some Companions: Roses, peony-flowered poppy, peonies
Primary Means of Spreading: Seeds
Aggressiveness: Moderate
Flowering Time: Late spring and summer

Stems 1 to 4 feet high and frilled with finely cut foliage are topped with elegant spires of white, blue, or pink flowers, which symbolize levity in the romantic language of flowers. Native to the Mediterranean region and naturalized in Asia, larkspurs have been enjoyed by mankind for centuries. At the National Herb Garden in Washington, D.C., they begin to flower as the old-fashioned roses are fading, blooming heavily in June. When the flowers mature to pods, ripen, and dry, they crack open with minimal handling to freely scatter small, irregularly angled seeds. The faded plants, their job done, can be relinquished to the compost pile, where they may encourage yet another crop of seedlings. Where seedlings are unwanted, they are easily unearthed.

Provide fertile, moist, well-drained soil. Cut the flower spikes when one-third of the flowers have opened, and the rest will unfurl indoors in a vase of fresh water.

COSMOS

(Cosmos bipinnata)

Hardiness: Annual
Exposure: Sun
Some Companions: Spider flower, ornamental grasses, shrub roses, coneflowers
Primary Means of Spreading: Seeds
Aggressiveness: Limited to moderate
Flowering Time: Summer and fall

Flamboyant, round, daisylike flowers of white, pink, or red stand 4 to 10 feet tall on strong stems clad in feathery leaves. In spring, cosmos emerge from seeds with gusto, stretching up to flowering size in just eight weeks. Natives of Mexico, they thrive in warm, frost-free weather. In addition to having a place in any cutting garden, cosmos are great fillers for open spaces between newly planted perennials or lanky shrub roses. They also can be used in large sweeps in meadow gardens. New flowers continue to open for several months, beginning at the stem tips and continuing alongside branches lower on the stem. When flowers are done blooming, they neatly drop the spent petals and get about the business of producing seeds.

For shorter plants, less prone to tipping in the wind, look for compact varieties, provide lean soil, and avoid high-nitrogen fertilizer.

Digitalis moriana, an unusual foxglove, has a pale apricot flower.

FOXGLOVE
(Digitalis purpurea)

Hardiness: Zones 4 to 8
Exposure: Light shade to sun
Some Companions: Bellflowers, anemones, cornflower, larkspur
Primary Means of Spreading: Seeds
Aggressiveness: Moderate to aggressive
Flowering Time: Late spring and early summer

Elegant spikes of pendulant tubular purple flowers with speckled throats look like exclamation points standing out in the garden. Foxglove grows 2 to 5 feet high, and the tallest forms can serve in the largest arrangement. Since most are biennials, freshly sown seeds sprout into low leafy rosettes the first year and flower the second year. Native to the western Mediterranean, they are naturalized in the United States and are considered an invasive pest in the Pacific Northwest.

Foxglove are poisonous plants from which the heart medication, digitalis, is extracted. They should be grown well away from foliage-eating pets or toddlers. Provide moist, fertile soil.

HARDY AGERATUM
(Eupatorium coelestinum)

Hardiness: Zones 5 to 10
Exposure: Sun to light shade
Some Companions: Chrysanthemums, reblooming daylilies, coreopsis, obedient plant, coneflowers, 'Autumn Joy' sedum
Primary Means of Spreading: Creeping stems and seeds
Aggressiveness: Aggressive
Flowering Time: Summer and fall

Beautiful clusters of blue flowers arise late in the growing season, when this color is a rarity. They resemble the powder-puff blooms of annual ageratums but stand 1 1/2 to 3 feet high and are great for cutting and drying. The foliage, attractive in its own right, is softly triangular and toothed. New plantlets sprout from creeping rhizomes to form large and far-reaching colonies for beautiful drifts of color when in bloom.

Originally, this native wildflower grew from Florida and the West Indies north to New Jersey but now is cultivated nearly nationwide. It thrives in moist soils—stream banks and well-irrigated gardens. Divide occasionally to keep hardy ageratum tidy.

ROSE CHAMPION
(Lychnis coronaria)

Hardiness: Zones 4 to 8
Exposure: Sun
Some Companions: Russian sage, purple coneflower, delphinium
Primary Means of Spreading: Seeds
Aggressiveness: Moderate to aggressive
Flowering Time: Summer

Over low rosettes of swirling, velvet silver foliage, flower stems rise 2 to 3 feet high, glistening with airy clusters of pink or sometimes white flowers. Acting as a biennial or short-lived perennial, rose champion begins flowering the second year and often sets seed and dies shortly thereafter, but not before spreading the seeds around. So aggressively does it seed that it can escape the garden and appear in disturbed soil nearby. Rose champion is native to northwestern Africa, southeastern Europe, and central Asia, the wide range showing its versatility. In the romantic language of flowers, it symbolizes deserving love.

Well-drained soil is a must, because like many silver-leaved plants, this one suffers in soggy soils. Wait until the entire flowering stem is in full bloom to cut it for an arrangement. You may have to clip off

59

fading terminal flowers but will have a better display of the remaining blossoms.

FLOWERING OR JASMINE TOBACCO
(Nicotiana alata)

Hardiness: Zones 7 to 10; annual farther north
Exposure: Light shade to sun
Some Companions: Petunias, salvia, love-in-a-mist, 'Flamingo Feather' celosia
Primary Means of Spreading: Seeds
Aggressiveness: Moderate to aggressive
Flowering Time: Summer and fall

Over large, lush, light green leaves reminiscent of fresh tobacco, lanky flowering spikes rise $1^1/2$ to 4 feet high. They bear pink, red, purple, or white trumpet-shaped flowers that are intensely fragrant at night, attracting night moths as well as daytime hummingbirds. The flowers mature into capsules brimming with tiny seeds that can self-sow with mouth-dropping abundance (see page 121). A South American native, this plant can be perennial in warm climates but usually is grown as an annual.

Like tobacco, these leaves are poisonous and should be kept out of reach of young children or pets. Provide moist soil and afternoon shade if wilting is a problem. Cut the flowers when fresh and plump in the morning or evening.

LOVE-IN-A-MIST
(Nigella damascena)

Hardiness: Annual
Exposure: Sun
Some Companions: Vining petunia, larkspur, foxglove, flowering tobacco
Primary Means of Spreading: Seeds
Aggressiveness: Moderate
Flowering Time: Summer

Furry and finely cut leaves spread below clear blue, pink, or white flowers that reach $1^1/2$ to 2 feet high. The flowers mature into inflated maroon-mottled seed capsules, handsomely cupped with frills of fine foliage. The flowers are suitable for cutting, and the seedpods are interesting for drying and using in everlasting arrangements and wreaths. Seeds, produced abundantly, are spicy flavored and sometimes used for seasoning. They tend to produce self-sown replacements if you allow some pods to mature, shatter, and spill their seeds.

These natives of northern Africa and southern Europe are easily started by direct-sowing fresh seeds in well-drained soil.

Shirley poppies flower in abundance in Don Vanderbrook's garden.

SHIRLEY POPPIES
(Papaver rhoeas Shirley Series)

Hardiness: Annuals
Exposure: Sun
Some Companions: Cosmos, peony-flowered poppy, California poppy
Primary Means of Spreading: Seeds
Aggressiveness: Moderate
Flowering Time: Summer

From a European wildflower that grew amid Roman ruins and European cornfields, Reverend W. Wilks of Shirley, England, bred the beautiful annuals we call shirley poppies. It was in the 1800s that he noticed wild corn poppies, which usually flowered in red, also appeared in pink outside the church garden fence. He saved seed from the most interesting plants to produce new and better colors—white, pink, rose, and red. The flowers arise from crooked stems 2 to 3 feet high, which straighten before the buds open. When done blooming, the entire plant dies, turning brown as the seed capsules dry and prepare to let loose the seeds. Seeds can scatter, arising in openings between pavement as well as between and around other plants. Leaving them unthinned in a tight cluster encourages the plants to stretch up taller before blooming, enhancing their virtues as cut flowers.

Shirley poppy petals, which look translucent and delicate, actually have a firm, crepelike texture, which is stunning in arrangements. To keep them looking good as long as possible, you need to seal the stem to prevent the milky sap from running out. Don Vanderbrook cuts newly opened flowers and immerses the bottom of the stems in boiling water for eighteen seconds to sear them shut. The seed capsules also can be used in dried arrangements.

Long-legged patrinia is an interesting newcomer to American cut-flower gardens.

PATRINIA
(Patrinia scabiosifolia)

Hardiness: Zones 5 to 8
Exposure: Sun
Some Companions: Asters, coneflowers, boltonia
Primary Means of Spreading: Seeds
Aggressiveness: Limited
Flowering Time: Summer and fall

Developed in Japan for the cut flower industry, eastern Asian patrinia has found its way to the United States in recent years. It has handsome, coarse, pinnate foliage that turns an attractive bronze in fall. In summer, patrinia sends up flowering stems to 3 feet high. They bear large, airy clusters of small yellow flowers that make wonderful fillers in the garden or vase. Usually

acting as biennials, they flower when two years old, set seed for a new generation, then die back.

Provide well-drained soil of moderate fertility. It can take several years of self-sowing to have flowering clumps established in the garden every year. Be patient.

NETTLE-LEAVED VERBASCUM
(Verbascum chaixii)

Hardiness: Zones 5 to 8 or 9
Exposure: Sun
Some Companions: Globe thistle, Russian sage, purple coneflower, catmint, ornamental grasses
Primary Means of Spreading: Seeds
Aggressiveness: Moderate
Flowering Time: Summer

A relative of the wild and somewhat weedy mullen, this plant first sports low-growing, silvery rosettes of foliage. When two years old, it stretches up into an impressive 3- to 6-foot-tall flowering spike that catches the eye in the garden or an arrangement. Yellow flowers with purple centers (also available in white-flowered forms) densely pack the stems and produce abundant seeds for self-sowing. Native to Eurasia, it is a hardy perennial.

A close relative, *Verbascum olympicum*, has yellow flowers on upright spires reaching up to 6 feet high. It is less hardy than nettle-leaved verbascum and may not thrive in colder climates, but is wonderful for cutting.

Both species grow easily in open soil with sharp drainage.

61

CHAPTER 4:
shaded woodland retreats

The rich wildflower flora of deciduous eastern woodlands has inspired free-spirited shade gardens across the country. With their teeming open-faced trilliums, dangling-blossomed Dutchman's breeches, and showy wood anemones, they symbolize spring abandon and beauty. Created where shade trees are mature, the sun is gentle, and the soil is deep and rich, eastern woodlands awaken and bloom in spring before tree canopies fill out. This is just when winter-weary eyes need them most.

Some of these wildflowers, able to spread into drifts or colonize any openings between protruding woody roots, have intriguing methods for conquering new territory. The most successful among them are

Dogwoods, azaleas, wood poppies, and Virginia bluebells sparkle in the spring woodland garden.

likely to put on the biggest and most beautiful displays. Wild ginger and mayapples, for instance, creep on rhizomes—carpeting the woodland with interconnected clones well able to grow independently if cut free. Woodland phlox walks on once-upright stems that arc to the ground, root, and sprout into a new plant that will also step out with arcing stems. Wild geraniums catapult their ripe seeds out of pods that snap open like a slingshot.

In spring, violets open smiling blossoms of violet, white, lavender, or yellow but in summer often replace them with petal-free flowers that will never open. Called cleistogamous, these flowers produce a multitude of seeds without regard for ordinary hazards such as lack of pollinators or foul weather. These reproductive schemes are put to good use when the plants are allowed to spread in a free-spirited garden.

When crickets begin their nightly serenade and tree leaves expand into an awning that covers the woodland garden with shade, the spring wildflower symphony subsides. Many spring wildflowers fade back to dormant roots, but some remain. Molded umbrella-shaped leaves of mayapples, colonies of wild ginger with their blanket of heart-shaped leaves, and fronds of ferns, arching up out of the ground like fountains, supply textured foliage that gives the garden quiet serenity. At the well-lit woodland edge, some summer bloomers show color. Tall meadow rue stretches 6 feet high and flutters billowing stamens. Red-flowered spikes of cardinal flowers open, sparkle, and draw jeweled hummingbirds.

There are, of course, woodlands in many regions of the country—all with their own interesting herbaceous flora. In the uplands or lowlands, coastal forests or floodplains, or anywhere dominant trees surrender space, sun, and soil for low-growing flowers, free-spirited wildflowers will come. And they will grow without special primping or coddling. These are very good reasons for including local species in your free-spirited woodland garden. Check wildflower sales at local nature centers or rescue wildflowers from construction sites. Be alert for them when they seek you out, emerging in your garden from wandering seeds when the conditions are right.

One fascinating example of a beautiful regional woodland community is found in Alaska, amid forests of birch and spruce on the southernmost tip of the Kenai Peninsula. In summer, when daylight reaches up to twenty hours, temperatures range between 50° F and 75° F, and rainfall is abundant, wildflowers grow with nearly tropical abandon.

Many Alaskan wildflowers are northern counterparts of plants common to the lower forty-eight states. Self-sowing chiming bells (*Mertensia paniculata*) has pink buds and blue flowers similar to Virginia bluebells (*Mertensia virginica*). Chiming bells, however, is unique—growing in the western United States and having bell- rather than trumpet-shaped flowers, a hairy stem, and more height than the eastern species. Melon berry (*Streptopus amplexifolius*) resembles smooth Solomon's seal (*Polygonatum biflorum*) with similar parallel-veined, oval leaves on graceful arching stems that hold white flowers dangling beneath. But melon berry produces juicy, sweet red berries, made into jellies by native Alaskans. The species capitalizes on berry-munching bears and other animals, which eat the showy fruit, wander off, and deposit the seeds in nutrient-rich droppings in new territory, an auspicious start.

Dwarf dogwood or bunchberry (*Cornus canadensis*), common as grass in much of Alaska but rare in parts of the northern United States, is a ground-hugging creeping shrub that reaches no more than 8 inches high. Its low-lying nature keeps it safe beneath the snow in winter. Bunchberry has oval leaves with arcing veins and white-bracted flowers that mature into red berries similar to those of the American flowering dogwood (*Cornus florida*). But the dwarf dogwood leaves are held in whorls

65

Woodland phlox spreads into open drifts of fragrant, bright, lavender-blue flowers.

instead of opposite pairs, and great contrasts in height make profound differences between the two.

Learn about your own unique native free-spirited plants, watching how and where they grow. Use these observations to create mini-communities of natural companions that look great in their shared habitat. Then, let the dance of life begin.

Donna and Ed Lambert stand amid the wood poppies in their woodland garden.

A Wildflower Garden Grows from Humble Beginnings

When Ed and Donna Lambert, a professor of art and his wife, moved into their riverside house in Athens, Georgia, twenty years ago, the wooded backyard slope leading to the floodplain was barren, eroding, and overrun with poison ivy and honeysuckle. Today there is a high-ceilinged hardwood forest rising above beds of wildflowers. In early spring, yellow-flowered woodland poppies stretch along perimeter beds. By late spring, lavender-flowered woodland phlox assumes control of the gardens by the house. Elsewhere masses of white-flowered Virginia waterleaf, lavender-blue—flowered scorpion weed and Virginia bluebells, and lanky clumps of red-flowered wild columbine come and go amid ferns, hostas, and more.

These plants luxuriate in rich soil, primed before planting by stock-piling neighborhood leaves for several years. As the heaps of leaves decays, the previously depleted soil grows moist, dark, and fertile—ideal for many woodland wildflowers.

The array of free-spirited woodland plants growing here were mostly begged, borrowed, or salvaged, then allowed to spread. Wildflowers and ferns were eased out of relatives' and friends' midwestern properties and transplanted to Georgia. Woodland phlox, taken from gardens left around a demolished house up the street, have expanded from six clumps to a mass 10 feet long. A small pack of Virginia bluebells, which took several

66

years to begin growing strongly, now have spread by seed into most of the beds, making sparkling patterns as their blue flowers appear here and there as far as the eye can see. Wood poppies, originally purchased as a three-pack from a discount store, advance aggressively, making large swaths and questing for ever more space.

On a road trip, the Lamberts rescued beautiful royal ferns (*Osmunda regalis*), with bright green fronds and rust-colored spore-bearing pinnae, from a death-dealing mower cutting a Carolina roadside ditch. These and other ferns reproduce not from seeds but from spores that grow into tiny patches of gametophytes, which in turn mate to grow into new ferns—a primitive two-phased reproductive cycle.

One of the Lamberts' favorite wildflowers is scorpion weed (*Phacelia bipinnatifida*), which grows well in mild climates (zones 6 to 8) and thrives in this Georgia site. This pretty little biennial, growing 1 to 2 feet high, has coiled clusters of lavender-blue flowers over lobed leaves and is particularly handsome when allowed to mingle in masses along the front of the garden. First-year plants produce foliage only. Flowers arrive the second

Ed and Donna Lambert's arching bridge leads over the pond.

Woodland phlox are among the showiest spring woodland wildflowers.

year. After the bloom is through and seed for the next generation has been scattered, the plants disappear.

Paths honeycomb the garden, skirting fallen trees, traveling beside interesting plant specimens, running along the Middle Oconee River, and circling to a reflective water garden. Once mere trails laid bare by repeated walking, they now are green with manicured turf or are paved in brick salvaged from an old railroad depot. Many walks are bordered with rock edgers to keep tautly pulled hoses from crushing nearby plants. Their graceful lines give the garden structure and purpose, carving what could be ordinary wilderness into man's domain.

The water garden, inspired by a friend's backyard pond, is complete with an arching bridge and small but musical waterfall, which gives the area a subtle Japanese garden ambience. The pond no longer contains schools of koi and other decorative fish, which became meals for wild river otters and great blue herons. But it does attract songbirds—eastern bluebirds, cedar waxwings, and others—who dive from the trees into the trickling waterfall.

Sculptural structures and accessories—a Japanese lantern, a bird-bath, potted plants, and artistic arrangements of boulders—add drama to the scene. Small understory trees such as dogwoods and Japanese maples arise in prominent places, adding their graceful artistry with picturesque trunks and horizontal branching.

The Lamberts like the beauty of their free-spirited wildflower garden and also appreciate that it helps nature return to a healthy balance. Each plant species nourishes or shelters a variety of insects, pollinators, and small plant eaters, who are, in turn, food for birds, bats, and other small carnivores. The smallest animals feed the owls and foxes in an interconnected cycle of life. Re-creating the foundation of nature's food web—the wildflowers and other native plants—gives all of this a start.

Native Ground Covers from American Woodlands

Two free-spirited ground covers that hail from opposite coasts illustrate the garden potential of little-known natives. Both are hardy, thriving in zones 5 to 8 and occasionally beyond, so are able to grow across much of the United States. Using large drifts of these plants, and a few other woodland creepers, is a great way to fill up a large shade garden with minimal expense and, at the same time, develop a simple but strong garden look.

Growing wild from Washington to California, vancouveria (*Vancouveria hexandra*) is a charming American twin to epimedium, a ground cover of Eurasian origin. Growing under 1 foot high, this rhizomatous creeper has leaflets shaped like duck's feet and airy white flowers that resemble fairy ballerinas to imaginative gardeners. Surprisingly hardy, it can grow as far north as Minneapolis.

Hailing from the eastern United States, spotted wintergreen (*Chimaphila maculata*) has whorls of elongated, evergreen leaves with showy white variegated veins spreading above creeping roots. Fragrant, nodding white or pink flowers add to the fun in summer. North Carolina plantswoman Edith Eddleman, who has fond childhood memories of

playing near this plant, twice enjoyed the good fortune of having the seeds delivered to her in bird droppings.

Horticultural Hints

As woodlands fall prey to subdivisions, the interest in preserving woodland natives in gardens has surged. But it takes more than planting to make a successful woodland garden. You need to replicate woodland soil—rich in decayed autumn leaves not found beneath trees growing in the lawn, on stiff clay left over after construction, or on parched sandy soils. Decayed leaves make the soil dark, moist, and fertile, the key to growing many wildflowers. If nature hasn't been building soil in your yard lately, you can mimic its work with generous additions of leaf compost, often available in bulk loads from municipal recycling departments.

Free-spirited wildflowers do not exist in a world unto themselves but are influenced by companion plants, and particularly by the trees

Rich soil nourishes foamflowers, wild geraniums, wild columbine, and wood poppies.

70

Learning More About Landscaping with Wildflowers

To make the most of wildflowers that creep into your shade garden, learn what makes them tick. Local botanical gardens, nature centers, or the Cooperative Extension Service (often found under federal or county offices in the phone book) may be able to help you. Or you can turn to national organizations that specialize in wildflower gardening. Consult the National Wildflower Research Center, 4801 LaCrosse Avenue, Austin, TX 78739-1702, or Wild Ones, P.O. Box 23576, Milwaukee, WI 53223-0576.

standing overhead and rooting down below. Groves of maples, for instance, yield quickly rotting leaves that build deep, moist topsoil. But maple canopies are dense and leave the forest floor dark once leaves expand in late spring. In the home landscape, sugar maples and silver maples often develop shallow, thick-spreading root systems liable to leave little rooting room for wildflowers. Oaks, which tend to be deep rooted, have open-branched canopies that let filtered light through and can support underplantings of summer- and fall-blooming woodland goldenrods or asters.

Remember there are wildflowers that will grow in nearly every bit of ground. So if you have carefully inventoried your garden site and choose to leave reasonably good-quality native soil unadorned, you can plant it with wildflower species well adapted to its special characteristics.

While many woodland wildflowers prefer moist, rich soil, you might have acidic, dry, and sandy soil. To get an idea of what plants would work well for this type of soil, look for a similar habitat, such as the dunes south of Lake Michigan. This is the home of wild lupines (*Lupinus perennis*), with handsome palmately lobed leaves and upright spikes of pea-shaped purple flowers, and bird's foot violet (*Viola pedata*), with finely cut leaves and dark-veined lavender flowers. Either one or both could work well for a free-spirited shade garden.

A little attention at strategic moments can help free-spirited woodland wildflowers thrive and spread. Although unlikely to flush golden with spring dandelions like sunnier spots, woodland gardens still will have their share of unsightly space-stealing weeds. If crabgrass and chickweed sneak in during fall or spring, pull them out by the roots before they go to seed and come up all over. To help in places where you want to discourage seed germination, cover bare earth with several inches of mulch. But where you want increasing drifts of a particular species, leave the nearby soil bare and plan to pull weeds by hand until the desired seedlings have taken hold of the space.

Because moisture, often so prevalent in spring, can become an issue in summer, it's handy to keep sprinklers available when drought strikes. Water deeply and as often as necessary to keep the soil evenly moist and prevent early dormancy of summer fillers, the persistent

Wood poppies often spread into drifts of abundant, and bright, yellow flowers.

foliage of mayapples, Virginia waterleaf, and others.

Structures with Natural Appeal

Woodland gardens offer many opportunities for blending free-spirited plants and architectural elements. A curving path can pass blushing masses of wild geraniums. A large rock might be edged by wood poppies. A bench can be surrounded by arching Solomon's seal fronds. Even a fallen tree can be cloaked with velvet moss and dripping with ferns and wildflowers. The combination of hard lasting structures and soft ephemeral wildflowers creates a dynamic mix. It also provides summer interest when prime spring players, like Virginia bluebells and scorpion weed, have gone underground until next year.

The Lambert's garden steps attract the eye and the imagination.

Paths offer more than a clearing for walking without tripping over logs and vines. They weave graceful lines around trees, giving the garden year-round form. To pave natural-looking paths, use bark mulch or wood chips. Begin by clearing away unwanted vegetation, laying folded sections of newspaper side by side over the barren earth, and covering the newspaper with several inches of mulch. Pull up occasional weeds that poke through and replenish the mulch annually.

Where the ground rises, you can cut the slope into a series of natural steps, getting into the spirit of the scene by using split tree trunks or natural cedar or redwood ties to hold up the steps. On a gradual slope, make the steps graceful—broad with a low rise. On a steep slope, steps will have to march more purposely with a taller rise and shorter step.

Glossary of Free-Spirited Woodland Flowers

The palette of woodland plants appropriate for your garden will vary depending on your site and climate. You can get ideas for wildflower combinations by noticing nature—the ferns that grow through and above may-apples, and other species that cooperate in close quarters. Free-spirited plants will soon begin making their own combinations, blending into compatible colonies. In addition to free-spirited wildflowers detailed below, you may want to try shade-loving free-spirited plants from other chapters.

WILD COLUMBINE
(Aquilegia canadensis)

Hardiness: Zones 3 to 8
Exposure: Partial shade to sun
Some Companions: Virginia bluebell, forget-me-nots, wild geranium
Primary Means of Spreading: Seeds
Aggressiveness: Limited
Flowering Time: Spring

Beautiful and graceful flowers are shaped like jester's caps with five upright red spurs over a yellow petticoatlike base with a little bush of golden stamens emerging beneath. They dangle on wiry branched stems to about 2 feet high. Hummingbirds

Wild columbine blends beautifully with golden-leaved hosta and forget-me-nots.

and bumblebees can reach nectar deep in the flower and are dusted with pollen, which they carry to the next flower. Flowers develop into upright sharp-tipped pods bearing many seeds for the next generation. When dry and brown, they crack open to spill out dozens of glossy dark seeds. The three-lobed leaflets are handsome and can look attractive through the growing season.

Provide well-drained soil, which doesn't have to be amended with extra organic material. Because parent plants will live only for several years, self-sown seedlings are important replacement plants. Plan to water during dry weather.

WILD GINGER
(Asarum canadense)

Hardiness: Zones 3 to 8
Exposure: Shade
Some Companions: Ferns, wood poppy, wild geranium, mayapple
Primary Means of Spreading: Creeping stems and seeds
Aggressiveness: Moderate
Flowering Time: Spring

Heart-shaped matte-finished leaves to 7 inches wide and 6 to 12 inches tall cluster in spreading colonies that look handsome at the edge of a wooded path or stretching beneath trees, shrubs, or tall perennials. In spring, look beneath the paired leaves for a rounded purple-brown flower set close to the ground. Although not attractive to most of us, the rotten meat colors look like heaven to early-rising beetles, flies, and other insects. To ensure cross-pollination with other plants, flowers first are female and then change to male. The flower develops into a capsule which, when ripe, disperses a new generation with unique genetic characteristics. Wild ginger also creeps on thick, ginger-scented rhizomes, once used medicinally. When the weather turns cold in fall, the deciduous leaves disappear until the next spring.

Native to the eastern United States, wild ginger is capable of growing across much of the country. Provide moist soil rich in organic matter.

WILD BLEEDING HEART
(Dicentra eximia)

Hardiness: Zones 3 to 9
Exposure: Shade
Some Companions: Wild ginger, blood-root, violets, foamflower, cardinal flower, daffodils, hostas
Primary Means of Spreading: Seeds
Aggressiveness: Limited
Flowering Time: Spring, summer, and fall

73

Wild bleeding heart, which has beautiful foliage and flowers that keep coming most of the growing season, is an outstanding free-spirited woodland plant. Above clumps of divided fernlike leaves, it produces small sprays of heart-shaped pink flowers reaching 10 to 18 inches high. Wild bleeding hearts look lovely in clumps beneath flowering shrubs and beside hostas and ferns, or in larger masses sweeping through a woodland garden. Flowers mature into seed capsules, lumpy with the wall-to-wall seeds developing inside. When the seeds are dark and ripe, the capsules spill them close to their parent, where the seedlings are easily found and moved. Seedlings may take only two years to begin flowering, a speed record among woodland wildflowers.

Wild bleeding heart, which grows naturally from New York to Georgia, thrives in rich, moist but well-drained soil, preferably of acidic nature. It can tolerate full sun in northern areas as long as the soil remains cool and damp. Irrigate during dry weather to prevent premature dormancy. A western counterpart, western bleeding heart (*Dicentra formosa*), naturally grows from British Columbia to California but can be cultivated across most of the country.

Wild geraniums edge a woodland walk.

WILD GERANIUM
(Geranium maculatum)

Hardiness: Zones 4 to 8
Exposure: Shade to sun
Some Companions: Wild blue phlox, false Solomon's seal, Virginia waterleaf, mayapple, purple trillium
Primary Means of Spreading: Creeping stems and seeds
Aggressiveness: Moderate
Flowering Time: Spring

This wide-spread, rhizomatous, native American wildflower has large, pale to rich-colored lavender or purple flowers emerging in open clusters over three to five parted leaves, and it grows to 2 feet high. It derives its common name, crane's bill, from the long, slender capsule that looks like a bird's beak when it emerges from a circlet of persistent white sepals. When the seeds are ripe, the capsule does a remarkable trick, surely one of the reasons for the plant's free-spirited success. It breaks into stringlike filaments that snap like a rubber band into coils, throwing the seeds away from the mother plant into new territory. Cross-pollinated flowers change from male to female so they cannot self-pollinate. Nectar deep inside the flower may be protected from dilution in the rain by the furry flower throat.

A widely adapted species, wild geraniums grow in open woodlands and can expand into sunnier areas as well. Provide moist, rich soil for best results.

VIRGINIA WATERLEAF
(Hydrophyllum virgatum)

Hardiness: Zones 5 to 8
Exposure: Shade
Some Companions: Jack-in-the-pulpit, wild ginger, wild geranium, wild blue phlox, Jacob's ladder
Primary Means of Spreading: Creeping stems and seeds
Aggressiveness: Moderate
Flowering Time: Spring and early summer

Handsomely divided leaves open with light silvery markings once thought to be watermarks from moisture dripped through the tree canopy. Reaching up to several feet high, white to violet bell-shaped flowers bristling with protruding stamens emerge in round clusters over the foliage. The creeping rhizome sprouts new growth along its length, expanding the colony the easy way. Native Americans reputedly ate new shoots, which accounts for common names like Shawnee-salad and Indian-salad.

Provide moist, organic-rich, and acidic soil. Keep plants constantly moist, watering during dry weather, to prevent premature dormancy.

CARDINAL FLOWER
(Lobelia cardinalis)

Exposure: Shade
Hardiness: Zones 3 to 8
Some Companions: Great blue lobelia, Joe-pyeweed, water iris, wild bleeding heart
Primary Means of Spreading: Seeds
Aggressiveness: Limited
Flowering Time: Summer

Spikes of rich red flowers rise on upright stems 3 to 4 feet high in midsummer when the woodland particularly needs color. The beautiful tubular blossoms open with protruding stamens designed to deposit their pollen on the head of visiting hummingbirds. The hummingbird, if nature's plan goes well, next will visit a slightly older flower, one that has finished shedding pollen and is prepared to act like a female.

74

Little round seed capsules, held close against the stem, mature to turn papery and brown. When the tiny seeds are ripe, the capsules pop open at the tip and seeds sprinkle out as the plant blows in the breeze or is brushed by passersby.

Cardinal flowers, which need rich, continually moist soil, often grow naturally in low wet areas or beside woodland streams. They require irrigation during dry weather. Because they are not a long-lived perennial, leave nearby soil clear after flowering to encourage self-sowing and development of new plants.

Masses of Virginia bluebells brighten a gray day.

Virginia Bluebells
(Mertensia virginica)

Hardiness: Zones 3 to 9
Exposure: Shade to sun
Some Companions: Wild ginger, wild blue phlox, spring beauty, Dutchman's breeches, troutlily, Virginia waterleaf
Primary Means of Spreading: Seeds
Aggressiveness: Moderate
Flowering Time: Spring

Virginia bluebells can grow into lavish colonies of 2-foot-high plants that show off cascades of dangling bell-shaped flowers and lush oval leaves. The flower buds swell, turn cool purple, open to lavender blue, and fade to light blue. Shortly after the last flower fades, the foliage begins to discolor and the show is over for the season. But seed development continues, as each flower produces four little nutlets, which are tossed to the ground as the failing stems flop. Where conditions are ideal, they may spread beneath deciduous trees and shrubs, even arising in a nearby lawn. Seedlings, which don't have a lot of growing time during their brief spring emergence, take several years to reach flowering size.

Provide rich, moist soil. Interplant with ferns, hostas, or other foliage plants to continue putting on a display after Virginia bluebells go dormant.

Wild Blue or Woodland Phlox
(Phlox divaricata)

Hardiness: Zones 3 to 8
Exposure: Shade to sun
Some Companions: Wild ginger, wild geranium, waterleaf, purple trillium
Primary Means of Spreading: Rooting stems and seeds
Aggressiveness: Moderate
Flowering Time: Spring

These lovely, low-growing wildflowers reach 1½ feet high and bear open clusters of light lilac flowers that form frothy masses where allowed to spread. The five-lobed trumpet-shaped flowers have a light fragrance and attract bees, butterflies, and hummingbirds. Flexible stems, clad in simple oval leaves, arch across the soil, sometimes rooting to form new plants. Self-sown seedlings are also abundant.

Wild blue phlox thrives in rich, moist soil, such as along wooded streams, but is quite tolerant of other conditions. It may expand out into grassy meadows or partly sunny gardens.

Mayapples push into a colony of wood poppies.

Mayapple
(Podophyllum peltatum)

Hardiness: Zones 3 to 9
Exposure: Shade
Some Companions: Virginia creeper, wild geranium, Virginia waterleaf, wood phlox, wood poppies
Primary Means of Spreading: Creeping stems and seeds
Aggressiveness: Aggressive
Flowering Time: Spring

Displaying large-lobed leaves paired into an umbrella-shaped plant about 1 foot high and wide, the mayapple and its aggressive rhizomes can colonize vast stretches of a woodland floor. It creates a beautiful and

75

uniform mantle of greenery. Unless you lift up a leaf, it will be difficult to see the nodding white flowers below. Possessing an unpleasant odor, they attract crawling beetles as pollinators. The entire plant is poisonous and unlikely to be eaten by deer and other herbivores, another reason for its success. Humans extract a drug, podophyllin, from the roots. While the immature fruit is toxic, the ripe yellow fruit (once called a hog apple) is nonpoisonous. It is designed to be eaten by woodland animals, which disperse the seeds in their droppings.

Provide moist, rich soil, and irrigation during dry weather. In cool climates, the leaves carpet the shade garden most of the growing season. In warm climates, they may fall dormant early. Mayapples also may be seen expanding into grassy areas and other unexpected places.

76

Variegated Solomon's seal, with its white-edged leaves, brightens a shady garden.

VARIEGATED FRAGRANT SOLOMON'S SEAL
(*Polygonatum odoratum* 'Variegatum')

Hardiness: Zones 4 to 9
Exposure: Shade
Some Companions: Jack-in-the-pulpit, wild geranium, bloodroot, liverwort, Jacob's ladder, foamflower
Primary Means of Spreading: Creeping stems and seeds
Aggressiveness: Limited to moderate
Flowering Time: Spring

This 3-foot-high Asian import has the beautiful arching stems of wild Solomon's seal plus creamy variegated edges that glow in the shaded garden through the summer. In spring, fragrant bell-shaped white flowers dangle beneath the leaves. They may attract pollinating bumblebees or may be self-pollinated to produce highly similar offspring. Flowers are followed by blue-black berries in the summer, which might catch the eye of a roving animal and be dispersed in its droppings. While many other Solomon's seal species go dormant after seeding, this variegated foliage can remain attractive until late summer or even fall. The most dramatic free-spirited movement comes as variegated fragrant Solomon's seal colonies expand on long rhizomes, making impressive clusters that stand out from a distance.

Provide rich, moist soil and irrigate to maintain consistent moisture in summer or chance early dormancy.

WOOD POPPY
(*Stylophorum diphyllum*)

Hardiness: Zones 4 to 8
Exposure: Shade
Some Companions: Wild geranium, Virginia waterleaf, mayapple, bloodroot
Primary Means of Spreading: Seeds

Aggressiveness: Moderate to aggressive
Flowering Time: Spring and early summer

Bold yellow flowers—with four large petals and a soft brush of multiple stamens—rise above handsomely lobed basal leaves. Native to the eastern United States, wood poppies are among the showiest of the spring-blooming woodland wildflowers. Like many members of the poppy family including the opium poppy, there often are surprises in the sap. In this case, it's yellow pigments. Plants can reach 12 to 20 inches high, and the foliage can persist much of the summer if the soil is kept moist. As flowers fade, they are replaced by bristly capsules to 2 inches long. The hundreds of small black seeds inside are released when the pods yellow and split. In the United States seedlings usually arise in abundance and can be moved easily when young. In Canada the wood poppy has been listed as extirpated, or no longer existing in the wild. Wild stands may have been overrun by an alien weed, garlic mustard (*Alliaria petolata*).

Wood poppy is similar to Eurasian celandine poppy (*Chelidonium majus*), an aggressive spreader naturalized in North America, but the latter grows to 4 feet tall and has orange sap. Provide rich soil and irrigate during dry weather.

TALL MEADOW RUE
(*Thalictrum polyganum*)

Hardiness: Zones 5 to 8
Exposure: Shade to sun
Some Companions: Virginia creeper, doll's eyes, cut leaf toothwort, Dutchman's breeches, wild geranium
Primary Means of Spreading: Seeds
Aggressiveness: Limited
Flowering Time: Late spring

Growing up to 8 feet high, tall meadow rue has airy sprays of green-tipped stamens that give a light, graceful look to the garden. The foliage is handsome and ferny. Unlike strictly insect-pollinated flowers with sticky pollen, meadow rue has abundant, light, dry pollen that can be caught by the wind and blown to neighboring plants. Some flowers dispense with the showy stamens and have only female organs.

Tall meadow rue, a native of the Eastern United States, grows in dappled sun at a woodland edge or along steam banks. It needs rich, moist soil, irrigated when the weather becomes dry.

FOAMFLOWER
(Tiarella cordifolia)

Hardiness: Zones 3 to 9
Exposure: Shade
Some Companions: Red maple, sugar maple, spice bush, jack-in-the-pulpit, wild geranium, great white trillium, false Solomon's seal
Primary Means of Spreading: Creeping stems and seeds
Aggressiveness: Moderate
Flowering Time: Spring

Foamy white flower spikes, reaching over 12 inches high, stand over the handsome maple-shaped leaves of this eastern United States native. Some cultivars, available in specialty catalogues, have burgundy foliage or pink flowers. Unlike many other woodland wildflowers that go dormant in summer, foamflower foliage may persist through the growing season and even turn autumn colors in fall. The many tiny flowers mature in spoon-shaped capsules topped with an upper lid. When ripe, the little dark seeds can slip off the spoon to the ground.

Foamflowers also creep on stolons, covering ground more quickly than they could from seedlings alone.

Provide moist, rich soil and an organic mulch of compost or leaves. Irrigate during drought.

MARSH BLUE VIOLET
(Viola cucullata)

Hardiness: Zones 3 to 8
Exposure: Shade to partial sun
Some Companions: Marsh marigold, jewelweed, skunk cabbage, Joe-pye weed, alexanders
Primary Means of Spreading: Creeping stems and seeds
Aggressiveness: Moderate to aggressive
Flowering Time: Spring and summer

Violets, which symbolize innocence and modesty, tend to be just the opposite—vigorous colonizers of well-suited sites. Just one of dozens of violet species that can spread through wooded gardens, the marsh blue violet native to the eastern United States has purple-blue flowers with a yellow center. The heart-shaped leaves stand about 6 inches high. The bearded floral throat allows honeybees, the preferred pollinators, to get a foothold on the petals. They push into the center of the flower, where pollen powders their abdomens, ready for transfer to the next flower visited. Seed set from the showy flowers is only one way many violets reproduce. As summer approaches, cleistogamous flowers appear. They look like buds and have no petals—they don't even open—but pollinate themselves and set scores of seeds. Reproduction is assured. The flowers, which are edible, were made into cold drinks or sautéed with lemon and orange by ancient Romans. Today, they are delightful to candy, by brushing with reconstituted powdered egg white and powdered sugar, and are used to decorate cakes and pastries.

This species prefers wet areas but other violet species are well suited to evenly moist or dry sites. Where well situated, some violets can become weedy and overbearing.

CHAPTER 5:
summer-celebrating prairie and meadow gardens

Sweeping stretches of tall grasses and
long-legged flowers display their summer
colors in meadows and prairies all across
the United States. Classic prairies, oceans
of grasses, sunflowers, asters, and other
forbs, once grew from Mexico to Canada,
east from the Rockies into the Midwest.
Herbaceous prairie plants thrived,
enduring long periods of drought, grazing
bison, and periodic fires by retreating
underground to perennial roots if necessary.
Shrubs and trees, less capable of regenerating when aboveground growth was
demolished, were prevented from rising
tall, stealing the sun, and slowly taking
over. Most prairie habitats have become
the domain of farm fields, livestock

*'Moonbeam' thread-
leaved coreopsis
angles behind a
self-sown clump of
'Goldilocks' annual
coneflower in the
author's garden.*

pastures, and residences, three good reasons to re-create this natural beauty in your own garden.

Meadows, often developed on old fallow farm fields, resemble prairies but are transient. Without drought and fire to maintain an herbaceous stronghold, they will eventually succumb to natural succession and become woodlands.

Meadows can contain a diverse mix of plants, but American prairies are composed of unique communities that vary with the growing conditions. In the Plains states, where winters are desperately cold and summers can be parched, the short-grass prairie predominates with grasses and flowers that may stay under a foot high. Farther to the east where rainfall increases, lusher stands of taller grasses such as prairie dropseed (*Sporobolus heterolepis*), side oats gramma (*Bouteloua curtipendula*), big bluestem (*Andropogon gerardii*), and little bluestem (*Schizachyrium scoparium*) gradually take predominance.

The star of many prairie gardens, little bluestem is one grass that you should be sure to include in a free-spirited meadow or prairie garden. Growing beautifully from Arizona to Maine and Quebec to Florida, it provides nonmotile clumps of handsome blue-green foliage, an attractive backdrop for other flowers. In fall, the leaves turn golden and linger much of the winter.

Because prairie and meadow gardens usually grow without need for herbicides, pesticides, fertilizers, and regular mowing, they are environmentally sound alternatives to intensively maintained lawns. They also create a more dynamic scene than never-changing clipped evergreens and turf, allowing homeowners to celebrate change as the seasons progress and free-spirited prairie plants blossom, seed, creep, and arise anew.

The prairie garden starts slowly in spring—late-blooming perennials arising reluctantly from their winter slumber. Use early prairie bloomers such as prairie smoke (*Geum triflorum*) and spiderwort, plus plants from a woodland edge, like woodland blue phlox, wild geraniums, and Virginia bluebells, as a warm-up for the plants that follow.

In midsummer, meadow and prairie perennials dominate the garden. Purple spikes of blazing stars stand at attention beside billowing flowers of grasses, which ripple in the breeze like waves on a beach. In moist meadows and roadside ditches, joe-pye weed stands 6 feet high and spreads impressive umbrella-shaped clusters of mauve flowers to the sun, drawing butterflies to its nectar and later small birds to its seeds. Golden, purple, and gray-headed coneflowers and also sneezeweed and sunflowers fill the garden with the look of daisies.

In autumn, green grasses turn golden and russet but remain alertly upright, often standing tall for the entire winter. Interesting clusters of velvet dark seed cones, all that's left of the many coneflowers, are supported on stiff stems. The seeds they harbor feed migratory birds and other small creatures, just as they have done in prairies for centuries.

If you have an open sunny location in your yard and crave this kind of experience, a prairie or meadow garden is a natural for you.

A Tall Prairie in a Small Lot

C. Coleston Burrell, author and landscape architect, lives in a century-old home on a modest city lot near downtown Minneapolis. His side yard includes only a token patch of lawn surrounded by plantings that replicate the prairie, woodland openings, and the mature forest.

A Blazing Star for Every Region

Blazing stars, summer and fall bloomers with tightly packed spikes of rose-purple flowers, are only marginally free-spirited but can spread by seed where conditions are right. Ideal requirements concerning temperature, moisture, and soil type vary with the species and influence in which part of the country they will thrive.

According to Neil Diboll, prairie ecologist and co-owner of the Prairie Nursery, prairie blazing star (*Liatris pycnostachya*) is most common in the Midwest. In moist eastern meadows, where rainfall is higher than the Midwest, you'll find spike gay feather (*L. spicata*), a popular garden plant. The harsh, dry Great Plains supports dotted blazing star (*L. punctata*), which stays neat and compact, typically hovering at about a foot tall. It has purple flower spikes feathered with long narrow leaves.

The prairie garden swells in the sunny opening adjacent to the city sidewalk, building a wall of greenery that provides privacy for the rest of the garden. Beside the sidewalk, a small planter set in a retaining wall holds glaucous, blue-leaved sea kale, an old-fashioned vegetable that contrasts dramatically with the 7-foot-tall naturalistic planting just above. The boulevard strip also bears traces of prairie plants—self-seeded coneflowers, goldenrods, blazing stars, and little bluestem.

To please neighbors during quiet moments in spring, Burrell plants tulips and daffodils that start the growing season off like any ordinary garden. He builds a classic mixed border framework of handsome foliage plants—creeping, furry, silver-leaved lamb's ears; self-sowing, mound-shaped, blue-green-leaved cushion spurge (*Euphorbia polychroma*); red-stemmed rhubarb; and variegated maiden grass. More color comes from pots blended with golden coleus, purple oxalis, green parsley, purple-flowered heliotrope, 'Limelight' helichrysum, and 'Herrenhausen' oregano.

Cole Burrell relaxes on the terrace in the woodland opening garden.

83

The garden takes a distinctively different turn by midsummer when meadow and prairie natives assume control. Cup plant, prairie dock (*Silphium terebinthinaceum*), and sneezeweed open bright golden daisylike flowers on lofty stems. Purple coneflowers and mauve heads of joe-pye weed (*Eupatorium purpureum* 'Atropurpureum') provide a cool comple- ment to the abundant yellows. Silky asters (*Aster sericeus*) change from large white flowers to plumed seeds that float away on the wind. A cluster of blue-flowered great blue lobelia (*Lobelia syphilitica*) has appeared on its own, perhaps coming unnoticed in another nursery pot, and staked a claim to a corner of the garden. Three gazing balls, round orbs with mir- rored purple surfaces, show the colors surrounding them like a fun- house mirror in a garden paradise.

Burrell, who has designed many authentic prairie plantings, enjoys pushing artistic limits by blending prairie and nonnative species in his garden. By layering short and tall, early- and late-blooming plants, he compresses dozens of species into a small area. Most contribute more than a pretty flower—they feed or shelter birds, butterflies, and other creatures, making a contribution to nature as well as man. The rich and

beautiful diversity contrasts strongly with more sterile contemporary landscapes monopolized by lawn and clipped evergreens.

Burrell's prairie garden is nearly sustainable, one step away from the wild prairie that grows and self-perpetuates independently. It lives without pesticides or herbicides but does benefit from occasional watering, weeding, and slug trapping. Ruled jointly by natural principles and man-made manipulations, it is one example of how free-spirited prairie plants and garden cultivars coexist in splendor.

A Meadow Garden at Longwood Gardens

Beautiful blends of native asters and goldenrods, escaped European wildflowers like hawkweed, Queen Anne's lace, and oxeye daisies, plus your own plantings of naturalizing self-seeders like cosmos, can make wild-looking meadow gardens for the back of your property, a sunny side yard, or anywhere you want a big, billowy look. When the meadow is in the public eye, it helps to surround it with a fence or cut through it with a path or boardwalk, to show that it is a well-loved garden and not the result of lawnmower failure.

One well-known meadow garden is at Longwood Gardens in

Kennett Square, Pennsylvania. The lavish former estate of Pierre du Pont, Longwood Gardens has twenty-two spectacular gardens, with formal roses, topiary, fountains, conservatories, and, on the perimeter, a meadow garden of grasses and wildflowers.

Originally a mowed field, the meadow was allowed to grow wild during the fuel crisis of the 1970s. While some handsome meadow flowers have found their way in naturally, others have been started with seed or transplants and left to survive and spread on their own.

Purple spikes of spike gayfeather (*Liatris spicata*) have seeded throughout one area to put on a big show in summer. Aggressively creeping goldenrods sweep across the land and light it up with golden flower plumes in late summer and early fall. New England asters, which spread by seeds, extend clusters of refreshing violet-blue flowers for autumn enjoyment. Saw-toothed sunflower (*Helianthus grosseserratus*), one of the most aggressive flowers, makes dazzling, large sweeps of golden daisylike flowers. In one low-lying wet area, purple-flowered violets have taken advantage of the moisture to carpet the swale and call it their own.

Asters, goldenrods, gayfeathers, and grasses are the stars of this garden. But their kingdom is threatened by weeds, unwanted woody creepers such as oriental bittersweet, Japanese honeysuckle, poison ivy, and raspberries that can resprout despite an annual early-spring burning and mowing that kills most trees and shrubs. These practices, combined with the thick growth of herbaceous meadow plants, helps prevent woody weeds from spreading excessively, says Robert Armstrong, Longwood research horticulturist. They probably are better than using herbicides, he theorizes, because the latter option leaves a gap in the meadow where more noxious invaders may infiltrate.

Spontaneous and free, this meadow provides natural relief for mowing and maintenance crews and visitors alike.

Great blue lobelia grows in clumps at the edge of a woodland bordering a meadow.

Washington State Palouse Prairie

The palouse prairie of eastern Washington and western Idaho took a much different form from the prairies of the Great Plains and Midwest. It arose on hills of rich, deep, moist, silty loam, was free from large grazing herbivores like buffalos, and was dominated by clump-forming blue bunch wheat grass (*Agropyron spicatum*) and Idaho fescue (*Festuca idahoensis*). Because these grasses can have difficulty regenerating after heavy livestock grazing, large portions of the prairie have disappeared. Other prairie lands have been stripped for cultivation of wheat, barley, legumes, and lentils. But when the hillsides were laid bare, the deep soils eroded away.

Little is left, except rare remnants of the charming free-spirited plants, a legacy finding its way into Pacific Northwest gardens. Dr. Benjamin Zamora of the University of Western Washington shared a few of the palouse prairie free-spirited perennials that he has grown and enjoyed in his garden.

Rosa woodsii is a pink- or white-flowered shrub growing to 6 feet high and spreading on creeping roots. Growing from northern Mexico through much of the West, the Great Plains, and even into Minnesota, it has potential for garden use in much of the United States.

Sticky geranium (*Geranium viscosissimum*), native from South Dakota to California, has large blue-purple or pink flowers that resemble cultivated geraniums, but are extraordinarily hardy.

A western form of bluebells (*Mertensia oblongifolia*) grows wild from Washington to Montana and northern California, spreading with seeds and rhizomes. It bears dangling blue flowers in spring and early summer. Although usually dormant by midsummer, the leaves may persist even longer if the plant is watered.

Many other species are finding their way into Pacific Northwest nurseries and offer exciting possibilities for the future.

Horticultural Hints

Prairie gardens with free-spirited flowers and easy-care grasses can become low-maintenance gardens once well established. The trick

A mowed walkway forms a focal point in the meadow at Longwood Gardens.

lies in starting out right. Seek out prairie plants that are well adapted to your climate and soil and keep them free from excessive competition by weeds—quack grass, dandelions, Canada thistles, and other strong competitors—until the soil is covered by desirable species. When well established, the prairie plants can hold their own.

It all begins before planting. Add extra organic material to difficult heavy or light soils. Eliminate as many weeds as possible by cultivating the soil several times. Till in fall or spring, allow several weeks for weed seeds to germinate, then hoe them down. If time permits, you can repeat this process, systematically eradicating most of the weed seeds stored up in the soil.

If you start a prairie garden from seed, expect to have to support it for several years before getting the free-spirited look you want. Another option is transplanting prestarted plants, spacing them about a foot apart. Although more expensive than seed, this can give good results within a year. If you keep the nursery labels beside the young plants, you'll be able to tell weed from free-spirited plant, a job that is not always easy to do when starting strictly from seed.

Sow prairie wildflower seeds in spring or early summer when the weather is warm. Nursery-grown perennials can be planted in spring, late summer, or fall. Mulch transplants with several inches of straw, helping keep the soil moist and reducing the germination of weed seeds.

Establishing a Natural Structure

One trick to creating a manageable prairie garden is to balance species with limited mobility like little bluestem and blazing star with free-spirited plants, says Jim Hagstrom, landscape architect and frequent prairie designer from St. Paul, Minnesota. Hagstrom suggests restricting the free-spirited self-seeders and creeping plants like black-eyed susans and anise hyssop to 30 percent of the garden. No matter where they arise from year to year, they will always have a handsome framework of grasses and other flowers around them.

If you have some gardening experience, you'll recognize notorious dandelions, thistles, and other common weeds when they emerge, and can hoe or pull them up before they become problems. If not, go to the library and check out a field guide with photographs of problem weeds to make their acquaintance before they show up in your garden.

Prairie plants tend to develop extensive root systems, one key to their success. When newly planted, they may seem to be growing slowly but actually are taking care of the business of root establishment before rising up tall. During the first two years of seeded prairie establishment, you can use the slow aboveground growth to your advantage. Mow the garden down several times the first year, setting your mower on its highest setting and cutting back weeds without harming prairie plants. Repeat this process the second year, using a string trimmer to cut back tall weeds at about 10 inches high. After a few years, when the prairie reaches its full height, you only need to pull out obvious weeds, using care not to disrupt prairie plants nearby.

Don't worry about fall cleanup in this garden. The seed heads of grasses and flowers can stand all winter, decorating the garden, feeding birds, providing a safe haven for wildlife, and self-sowing. Prolific seeders, like annual black-eyed susans, can move around from year to year,

Purple cone-flowers offer long-lasting color.

sprouting up in new openings to form changing drifts and patterns.

While prairie parks are usually burnt once a year to give the plants a fresh start and eliminate woody plants, you may not want to do that in your garden. Instead you can mow in early spring, preferably using a mulching mower to chop up old debris. Alternatively, you could use a string trimmer to cut vegetation down, rake it up to compost, and return the organic matter to the garden once decayed.

Getting Centered with Boardwalks

One of the best ways to appreciate a free-spirited prairie garden is by wandering right through the middle on a boardwalk. You can watch the butterflies and birds play and the tall grasses blow in the breeze without crushing plants or compressing the soil.

A boardwalk also allows you to put some structure into the garden. You can make the walk reflect the architecture of the house—mimicking the angles of the entryway or a nearby bay window. The boardwalk has a handsome stability as plants move and change, achieving an ideal balance in a free-spirited garden. For comfort and durability, make the board-walk at least 3 feet wide and use rot-resistant timbers.

A boardwalk provides access and design definition in Fred Rozumalski's garden.

Glossary of Prairie and Meadow Plants

Here is a delightful assortment of prairie and meadow plants for sunny free-spirited gardens.

NODDING ONION

(Allium cernuum)

Hardiness: Zones 3 to 9
Exposure: Sun
Some Companions: Purple coneflower, golden coneflower, blazing stars, grasses
Primary Means of Spreading: Seeds
Aggressiveness: Moderate
Flowering Time: Summer

To break up the near monopoly that daisy-like flowers have on the meadow and prairie garden, add some flowering onions. Nodding clusters of white or pink flowers stand 1 to 2 feet high above linear onion-flavored leaves, which remain green through the summer. After the flowers fade, starlike dried seed heads, attractive and prolific, develop and produce abundant seeds and plenty of offspring. Nodding onions also reproduce by multiplying bulbs, covering ground more slowly than the seeds but providing easy opportunities for propagation by division.

Growing from the east coast to the west coast, this plant is very versatile when provided with average to fertile, well-drained soil.

BUTTERFLY WEED

(Asclepias tuberosa)

Hardiness: Zones 3 to 9
Exposure: Sun
Some Companions: Violet sage, artemisias, joe-pye weed, blazing stars, sunflowers
Primary Means of Spreading: Seeds
Aggressiveness: Limited
Flowering Time: Summer

Native American butterfly weed embodies many great attributes of free-spirited prairie plants. It grows 2 to 3 feet tall and has a deep taproot that keeps the heart of the plant safe underground. Large flat-topped clusters of brilliant orange flowers bloom long into the summer, attracting all manner of butterflies. Newer cultivars are available with yellow or red flowers as well as orange. The flowers are structured so that visiting insects snag a saddlebag of waxy pollen clusters on their legs when leaving and disperse them to fertile pollen traps on other flowers. Seeds are mobile, breaking out of narrow pods and catching the breeze with fluffy plumes of silk.

Some other milkweed species for prairies and meadows include 5-foot-tall pink-flowered swamp milkweed (*Asclepias incarnata*) and 3-foot-tall showy milkweed (*Asclepias speciosa*), which can creep to form impressive colonies.

Butterfly weed requires only well-drained soil and freedom from root disturbance to grow well in many climates.

Volunteer heath asters surround a cultivated aster.

HEATH ASTER

(Aster ericoides)

Hardiness: Zones 3 to 9
Exposure: Sun
Some Companions: Goldenrods, New England aster, patrinia, hardy ageratum
Primary Means of Spreading: Creeping stems and seeds
Aggressiveness: Moderate
Flowering Time: Fall

This charmer, a personal favorite, makes great clouds of small, white, yellow-centered flowers while most other flowers are fading. Cultivars are available with flowers of pink or blue. Heath aster naturally grows 1 to 3 feet high, but when cut back it may stay only inches high and still have an endearing covering of bloom. A graceful mound-shaped plant, heath aster has small narrow leaves and usually sheds the basal leaves before flowering. Seeds develop a fluffy pappus that helps them blow to new domains and escape the mother plant. They also spread on slowly creeping rhizomes, which are easily unearthed where unwanted.

Heath aster tolerates a wide range of growing conditions, as it grows wild from the Great Plains to northern Mexico and the east coast. Provide average or moist soil.

NEW ENGLAND ASTER

(Aster novae-angliae)

Hardiness: Zones 3 to 8
Exposure: Sun
Some Companions: Goldenrods, sunflowers, coneflowers, chrysanthemums, hardy ageratum, turtlehead
Primary Means of Spreading: Seeds
Aggressiveness: Moderate
Flowering Time: Late summer and fall

The name for the genus *Aster* comes from the Greek word for *star*, referring to the many bright florets that beam out from a single flower head. Although asters represent unpredictability in the romantic language of flowers, some of the wild native asters are among the most durable and reliable of perennials. The New England aster, which grows from the east coast to the Great Plains, is one of the most spectacular fall bloomers. It has irridescent purple, yellow-centered flowers that attract butterflies and contrast nicely with all the golden fall flowers—mums, goldenrods, and coneflowers. Cultivated forms come in many additional flower colors—purple, pink, and red. The species spreads by seeds, developing many of them, though not all are viable. New England aster grows 3 to 5 feet tall and has elongated leaves with stem-hugging leaf bases.

These asters grow best in moist, even heavy soils. In highly fertile garden soils, they can become lanky and floppy. For more compact growth, pinch plants back in early summer. Divide frequently for peak performance. To try a companion aster capable of creeping into large clumps, consider growing the east coast New York aster (*Aster novi-belgii*), also parent of many modern cultivars.

LANCE-LEAVED COREOPSIS
(*Coreopsis lanceolata*)

Hardiness: Zones 3 to 8
Exposure: Sun
Some Companions: Purple coneflower, black-eyed susan, goldenrods, asters, daylilies, yarrow
Primary Means of Spreading: Seeds
Aggressiveness: Moderate
Flowering Time: Summer and fall

Lance-leaved coreopsis has a bold golden flower.

Growing in meadows, prairies, or the edges of woods, this native American coreopsis is a durable, sunny flower with an exceptionally long period of bloom. Reaching 1 to 2 feet tall with lance-shaped leaves, it spreads golden daisylike flowers on narrow willowy stems suitable for cutting. The narrow 1/8-inch-long seeds can blow a short distance and sprout up in new territories.

Many other coreopsis species also are worth growing. Similar large-flowered coreopsis (*Coreopsis grandiflora*) can be grown beside or instead of *C. lanceolata*. Thread-leaved coreopsis (*C. verticillata*), graceful native to the southeastern United States, spreads with slowly creeping underground stems and seeds. Annual calliopsis (*C. tinctoria*) is a freely self-sowing annual that can grow to 4 feet tall and bears yellow-edged dark-centered flowers.

Grow coreopsis in well-drained, average to light soil. They can tolerate drought once established. Flowering will continue most profusely if you remove the old seed heads, but free-spirited seeding will be minimized.

PURPLE CONEFLOWER
(*Echinacea purpurea*)

Hardiness: Zones 3 to 8
Exposure: Sun to partial sun
Some Companions: Black-eyed susan, coreopsis, goldenrods, asters, butterfly weed, rattlesnake master
Primary Means of Spreading: Seeds
Aggressiveness: Moderate to aggressive
Flowering Time: Summer

This purple-flowered American native grows naturally in the Midwest and central states and is a pleasant counterpart to the many golden daisy-shaped flowers. It reaches 3 or 4 feet high with a taproot, hairy leaves, and drooping rose or mauve florets around an elevated orange central cone. The flowers, which bloom through much of the summer, attract butterflies. The seeds, 3/8-inch-long and shaped like a rocket capsule, begin to come loose from the cone about four weeks after flowering and can shake free if you wait until then to deadhead. If you leave the cones on for winter interest, expect to find an abundance of little leafy seedling clumps arising nearby in spring.

Provide well-drained, average, moist, or lean soil. Once established, purple coneflowers can tolerate drought with the best of them.

93

QUEEN OF THE PRAIRIE
(Filipendula rubra)

Hardiness: Zones 3 to 9
Exposure: Sun to partial sun
Some Companions: Joe-pye weed, asters, blazing stars, turtlehead, goldenrods
Primary Means of Spreading: Creeping stems
Aggressiveness: Aggressive
Flowering Time: Summer

Growing wild across the eastern states, into the Midwest, and escaping from gardens in other regions, this is a bold free-spirited perennial with many regional affiliations. The plants grow 3 to 6 feet tall and have long compound leaves and airy sprays of aromatic pink flowers in summer. Although not long lasting, they make nice cut flowers. As with astilbes, you can leave the feathery faded flower plumes for fall and winter interest. Short underground stems, which run under the soil surface, emerge to sprout leafy rosettes, each of which can mature into a full-fledged new plant able to expand similarly.

Thriving in moist soil, queen of the prairie is good to use near drainage ditches, ponds, streams, or low wet areas. In a garden setting, enriching the soil with extra organic material and irrigating to keep it moist will encourage spreading. Divide as needed to maintain some order.

PRAIRIE SMOKE
(Geum triflorum)

Hardiness: Zones 1 to 7
Exposure: Sun to partial sun
Some Companions: Hardy geraniums, bird's foot violet, pasque flower
Primary Means of Spreading: Seeds
Aggressiveness: Limited
Flowering Time: Spring and early summer

To bring early color to a prairie garden, consider this interesting compact plant, ideally used for the front of the garden. Neat divided leaves are topped by flower stalks under 1 foot high, bearing small pink flowers and purple bracts. The plant really shines when the flowers fade and seed heads develop to look like long, furry, smoky plumes. Growing widely in nature, it is found from the Rocky Mountains to the northern tundra and across the Midwest deep into the East.

For best results, provide well-drained soil and a cool setting.

SNEEZEWEED
(Helenium autumnale)

Hardiness: Zones 3 to 8
Exposure: Sun
Some Companions: Joe-pye weed, spiderwort, turtlehead, New England aster
Primary Means of Spreading: Seeds
Aggressiveness: Limited to moderate
Flowering Time: Late summer and fall

Growing across the eastern and central states, this wildflower makes a big bright show in moist places. Abundant flowers, with drooping golden or yellow, scallop-edged florets surrounding a yellow or brownish disk, stand 3 to 5 feet high. The stems tend to be winged, an easy identification characteristic.

Where soils are less than rich and moist, plan to irrigate during dry weather. Because the lowest leaves may drop, surround a planting with interesting lower growers such as hardy ageratum. If self-sown seedlings are overabundant, dead-head to reduce seed set and you may be rewarded with additional flowering.

MAXIMILLIAN SUNFLOWER
(Helianthus maximillianii)

Hardiness: Zones 3 to 8
Exposure: Sun
Some Companions: Coneflowers, asters, hardy ageratum, coreopsis
Primary Means of Spreading: Seeds
Aggressiveness: Moderate to aggressive
Flowering Time: Late summer and fall

There are many species of sunflowers, including the cultivated annual described on page 131. Ask at a local nature center to find out which species are native to your area and consider adding them to your garden. Maximillian sunflower, a magnificent perennial, also is worth growing for its dramatic displays of thickly clustered, yellow daisy-shaped flowers. The petal-like structures in each of the flower heads are individual flowers and can be capable of producing seed, providing potential for self-seeding abundance. Growing up to 9 feet tall, Maximillian sunflower bears narrow, opposite leaves that can reach 12 inches long. Native from Texas to Minnesota and farther west, the species recently has naturalized in eastern states.

A versatile plant, Maximillian sunflower naturally grows in lean sandy soils but also thrives in average to moist garden soil.

FALSE SUNFLOWER
(Heliopsis helianthoides)

Hardiness: Zones 3 to 9
Exposure: Sun
Some Companions: Butterfly weed, blazing stars, chrysanthemums, purple coneflower
Primary Means of Spreading: Seeds
Aggressiveness: Moderate
Flowering Time: Summer

This flower typifies summer and is native to the eastern and central United States. With opposite, triangular, toothed leaves on stems 3 to 5 feet high, it spreads airy clusters of solitary, daisylike heads of yellow florets. These clustered florets attract a variety of bees, butterflies, and other pollinators that can visit dozens of tiny florets in each flower, an all-you-can-eat buffet strategy. False sunflower doesn't dally when it comes to reproduction by seed. Seedlings grow and become established so quickly that they may flower the same year they sprout if allowed an early start and long growing season.

False sunflower grows in almost any soil but stays most compact where the soil

Evening primroses have typical golden flowers in an atypical shape.

is not overly fertile. Water during dry weather to prevent wilting. Deadheading will encourage repeated bloom, but allowing seed formation will produce more seedlings. Take your pick.

MISSOURI EVENING PRIMROSE
(Oenothera missourensis syn. O. macrocarpa)

Hardiness: Zones 4 to 8
Exposure: Sun
Some Companions: Blazing stars, hardy geraniums, asters, yarrows
Primary Means of Spreading: Creeping stems and seeds
Aggressiveness: Moderate
Flowering Time: Summer and fall

If there are not yet enough yellow flowers in the garden, here is another to consider. It differs from all the others in having open cup-shaped four-petaled flowers that can measure up to 5 inches across. The name, evening primrose, was inspired by the flower's opening at night to attract pollinating moths. Upright or trailing stems can reach 20 inches long and are clad in light green, narrow leaves.

Although Missouri evening primrose is native to a relatively small area, from Missouri and Kansas south to Texas, it thrives in many climates and grows nicely in rich or average soils. Once well established, it will tolerate drought with minimal irrigation.

Gray-headed coneflowers and wild bee balm blend in the Hagstrom garden.

GRAY-HEADED CONEFLOWER
(Ratibida pinnata)

Hardiness: Zone 3 to 9
Exposure: Sun
Some Companions: Butterfly weed, blazing stars, yarrows, queen of the prairie, grasses, wild bee balm
Primary Means of Spreading: Seeds
Aggressiveness: Moderate
Flowering Time: Summer

This freely self-sowing prairie native is a favorite for prairie restorations. Showy, drooping yellow florets surround a large, round, purple-brown cone on plants that can reach 4 feet high. In fall, after the showy florets drop, the cone turns gray, thus giving the plant its common name. The pinnately divided, rough-textured leaves form low clusters and grow sparingly on the stem. These characeristics provide an easy way to distinguish this plant from similar-looking coneflowers and sunflowers.

Gray-headed coneflowers tolerate a wide variety of conditions, from dry to average and rich soils. Rich soils, however, are likely to encourage flop-prone plants.

95

GOLDEN CONEFLOWER
(*Rudbeckia fulgida*)

Hardiness: Zones 3 to 9
Exposure: Sun
Some Companions: Violet sage, Russian sage, 'Autumn Joy' sedum, blazing stars, asters, purple coneflower
Primary Means of Spreading: Seeds
Aggressiveness: Moderate
Flowering Time: Summer and fall

If there is one plant that has drawn attention to the idea of meadow and prairie gardening, it's the golden coneflower. A long-blooming easy-care flower that is used in sweeping masses in perennial gardens, golden coneflower is a prairie native with special distinction. The flowers, which have golden florets around a small black cone, can bloom for much of the summer. The dark cones, held upright on sturdy stems, offer food for birds and look attractive much of the fall and winter. Golden coneflower has furry oval leaves and reaches 1½ to 3 feet high.

Golden coneflowers grow easily in average to moist, well-drained soil. Occasional division for rejuvenation and propagation can be warranted.

BLACK-EYED SUSAN
(*Rudbeckia hirta*)

Hardiness: Zones 2 to 9
Exposure: Sun
Some Companions: Mullen, yarrows, goldenrods, ox-eye daisy, purple coneflower, coreopsis
Primary Means of Spreading: Seeds
Aggressiveness: Moderate to aggressive
Flowering Time: Summer

Some of the most floriferous perennials have only a short lifespan. That is the situation with the black-eyed susan, which sometimes acts like an annual or biennial. Fortunately, it produces enough seed to replenish its numbers in free-spirited gardens. Narrow upright plants reach to 3 feet high, bearing modest-sized golden florets around a dark purple-brown center. They are excellent for cut flower arrangements. Once seed is set, the plants quickly begin to look shabby and may be thinned out, leaving a few of the best to seed. Seeds begin to fall free once cones change to gray and begin to loosen up. The furry-leaved seedlings are easy to recognize.

Originally from the Midwest, this self-sower has spread throughout the United States and into southern Canada and northern Mexico. It grows well in average to moist but well-drained soil and can tolerate drought. In lean soils, it is less likely to flop.

Cup plant flowers in the garden of Ruth Stein, a Wild Ones member who has converted most of her backyard into a prairie garden.

CUP PLANT
(*Silphium perfoliatum*)

Hardiness: Zones 3 to 8
Exposure: Sun
Some Companions: Joe-pye weed, purple coneflower, blazing stars, sunflowers, asters
Primary Means of Spreading: Seeds
Aggressiveness: Moderate
Flowering Time: Summer

Cup plant flowers, like so many others, are yellow daisies that reach up to 8 feet high. The central disk flowers, unlike most in the sunflower family, are sterile and unable to produce seeds. That job is left to the showy outer-ray florets. What makes this perennial visually distinctive are the leaves, which arise in opposite pairs and sweep around the stem to form a cup.

Cup plant requires moist, fertile soil for best performance. Seedlings take some time to reach flowering size, first establishing a deep taproot and then rising high to bloom.

ROUGH-STEMMED GOLDENROD
(*Solidago rugosa*)

Hardiness: Zones 4 to 9
Exposure: Sun
Some Companions: Asters, boltonia, ironweed, blazing star
Primary Means of Spreading: Creeping stems and seeds
Aggressiveness: Aggressive
Flowering Time: Fall

Goldenrod, which blooms simultaneously with nondescript allergy-invoking ragweed, is often blamed for late summer hay fever. It, however, is not the culprit. Pollinated by a variety of insects, goldenrod pollen is heavy and sticky, not suitable for blowing in the wind and irritating people. Rough-stemmed goldenrod has graceful, golden flower plumes. Growing to 6 feet high, it spreads with rhizomes and can self-sow. The seeds develop with a fluffy pappus, which may help them catch the wind. During summer, the lower leaves may drop, but in fall, basal rosettes sprout to spend winter low to the ground.

Plant in any average, well-drained soil where this plant has room to run.

Common Spiderwort
(*Tradescantia virginiana*)

Hardiness: Zones 4 to 9
Exposure: Sun to light shade
Some Companions: Beard tongue, purple coneflower, wild bleeding heart, joe-pye weed, turtlehead
Primary Means of Spreading: Creeping stems, sagging stems, and seeds
Aggressiveness: Moderate to aggressive
Flowering Time: Late spring and early summer

Common spiderwort, which grows 1 to 3 feet high, brings welcome early color to the meadow and prairie garden. The blue, purple, and occasionally pink or white flowers have three large petals. Linear leaves can reach a foot long and an inch wide. Flowering for as long as four weeks, new blossoms open in the morning and close in the afternoon, with many new buds waiting in the wings to take their place. Common spiderwort sets enough seed to self-sow nicely, and sometimes aggressively. Rhizomes or stolons produce new leafy clumps to claim more territory for the mother plant. Slouching stems that root where they touch the ground also meander across the garden.

This plant is widely adapted and easily grown in average to moist soil. It spreads most quickly where fertility is high. Water during drought and have patience if the plant dies back or needs to be cut back in summer to return in fall.

Golden Alexanders
(*Zizia aurea*)

Hardiness: Zones 3 to 9
Exposure: Sun to light shade
Some Companions: Butterfly weed, columbine, shooting star, hardy geraniums
Primary Means of Spreading: Seeds
Aggressiveness: Moderate
Flowering Time: Spring and early summer

This flower, native from Quebec to Florida and Texas, conveniently blooms early in the season when color is needed most in a meadow or prairie garden. Umbrella-shaped clusters of tiny yellow flowers appear over 1- to 2½-foot-tall stems clad in divided leaves. They can spread in moist areas to cover the land like a golden cloud in May. As they do on many members of the dill family, swallowtail and other butter-flies often rear their caterpillars on this plant.

This plant grows best in moist soils, living in prairies, woodlands, savannas, and floodplains.

CHAPTER 6:
gardening in gravel

Paths and sitting areas, paved easily, inexpensively, and beautifully with gravel, are eligible to become free-spirited gardens in their own right. During warm rainy weather, gravel encourages prolific germination of a variety of free-spirited volunteers such as forget-me-nots and sweet alyssum. Airy and light during dry seasons, gravel also can cater to plants that need sharp drainage—Mediterranean herbs, succulents from arid climates, and drought-tolerant flowers. Dry at the top and moist and cool below, gravel can appeal to alpine plants such as mountain-dwelling bluebells (*Campanula spp.*), pinks (*Dianthus spp.*), and saxafrages (*Saxafraga spp.*).

Dame's rocket flowers beside bearded iris and forget-me-nots in Valerie Strong's garden.

Gravel, made up of uniform pieces of round stone $3/8$ to $1/2$ inch in diameter, exceeds the particle size of sand, silt, or clay, the most common components of garden soil. Because the rounded stones are unable to fit tightly together, excess moisture has many channels to flow in and out. Air penetrates easily, providing an oxygen- and carbon dioxide–rich subterranean environment preferred by the plants mentioned above. Gravel also acts like a mulch—coating the earth's surface, moderating temperature changes, and reducing evaporation so the lower layers of gravel and soil tend to stay cool and moist.

In the moist, cool weather of spring, a gravel garden might be crowded with sky-blue sprays of forget-me-nots accompanying golden trumpeted daffodils. In a slightly shaded gravel garden, lady's mantle (*Alchemilla mollis*) can flourish. This hardy self-seeding perennial unfurls dainty lobed, toothed leaves covered with downy hairs that hold morning dew like glittering diamonds on pedestals. Small frothy sprays of chartreuse flowers appear in spring, elegant when draped languidly against a bed of gravel. Should the earth become too dry, the lady is quick to complain as her leaf margins will turn brown and crisp, a signal more irrigation is needed.

Many of the free spirits introduced in other chapters will grow happily here. Cut flowers like self-sowing poppies, rose champion, and verbascums are naturals. Wandering perennials like yarrow, snow-in-summer, and creeping sedums, and also herbs like artemisia, bronze fennel, oregano, lamb's ears, and thyme, make themselves right at home. In the Midwest, sunflower seedlings can sprout from winter bird seed scattered by picky northern cardinals.

In warm climates, a gravel garden is ideal for tender drought-tolerant perennials. In coastal California, fragrant Spanish lavender (*Lavandula stoechas* subsp. *peduncula*) can self-sow in or beside gravel gardens. It becomes a bushy shrub with elongated gray leaves, topped with long-stalked purple flowers, all delightfully fragrant.

When silhouetted in the sun against a green lawn and other vegetation, graveled areas stand out brightly—much more so than the dark

bark-mulched paths preferred in naturalistic woodland gardens. For this reason, gravel makes a dynamic stage for showcasing free-spirited plants. You might use it for a garden walk, an access path to the compost pile, or an opening for a picnic table and grill, creating a unifying color rhythm in the yard. Add perimeter drifts of free-spirited plants—thyme, fennel, calendula, and verbascum—to soften barren expanses and bring them to life.

101

The idea of using gravel in the garden is nothing new. It is an essential component of Japanese contemplation gardens with their seas of raked gravel flowing around green islands of evergreens and moss, a combination designed to allow the mind to relax and move on to a higher plane. In England, writer and gardener Vita Sackville-West created gravel gardens for creeping and wooly thyme. John Brookes, contemporary British landscape designer and author, uses gravel as a form of soft surfacing that goes hand in hand with self-seeders.

In the interest of free-spirited gardening, gravel has much to offer.

Forget-me-nots, creeping phlox, lily-flowered tulips, and creeping sedum greet passersby at Valerie Strong's house.

A Midwestern Gravel Garden

Gravel walks—woven around gardens, decorative ponds, and gathering areas, all romantically clad in self-seeding and creeping flowers and foliage—have been a hallmark of Valerie Strong's garden for the past two decades. The quarter-acre property in Hudson, Ohio, has one of the finest free-spirited gardens in the country.

Strong is a garden designer educated in Europe and influenced by John Brookes, James Van Sweden, and Mien Ruys, all of whom take an interest in naturalistic styles of planting. Her ideas have a unique twist,

however, as shown in her garden, which straddles the boundary between wild and cultivated and emphasizes the singularly charming contrasts between the two.

The front yard is a small space about 25 feet deep, raised above eye level from the street with a tiered retaining wall made of salvaged barn foundation stones. The retaining wall billows with free-spirited flowers such as pink- and white-flowered columbine, thyme, pink rockcress, and old-fashioned wild petunias that flower in an array of pinks and mauves. The front of the house is shaded by a large spruce tree, but the opening beside it features a small pond, filled with water lilies and surrounded by a gravel sitting area. Running drifts of bee balm and self-sowing coreopsis, forget-me-nots, portulaca, garden heliotrope, and feverfew emerge here and there in the gravel and crowd around Greek and Mexican containers brimming with annuals.

A single balloon flower, with swollen flower buds like hot air balloons and open bellflowerlike blossoms, is a lonely remnant of the original formal garden that has survived in this place despite burying, cutting, and digging. Foliar clusters of purple smokebush, paper bark maple, and maiden grasses provide a stable backdrop to the garden.

Even more impressive gardens await review in the backyard. A brick patio is framed by a post-and-beam-type arbor made of locally cut locust poles and draped with pole beans and self-sowing heirloom morning glories. Beyond it gravel paths lead off through abundant flowers to a potting shed, made of rough timbers and a thatched roof, two water gardens, a kitchen garden, and a summer house. The summer house, built of weathered lumber, has a deck overlooking one pond, cushions for summer lounging, a sleeping loft, and a tin roof to play the music of falling rain. It is draped in fragrant climbing roses.

Ducks and other wildlife make themselves at home.

The water gardens, banked in rocks and filled with such denizens of wet and boggy areas as marsh marigolds and yellow creeping jenny, are tranquil attractions. They reflect the flowers around and attract wild ducks and dragonflies, even though the garden is a stone's throw from the center of town. Big balloon-throated bullfrogs charm nighttime visitors with their huge croaking calls. American toads liven up spring evenings with long chirping trills and evening orgies. A dry stream bed is made of clusters of cobbled rocks embedded in a shallow slope with creeping thyme, miniature pinks, pink evening primroses, and more along the banks.

Despite the small size of the property, there is enough to keep one's attention for hours. In the garden beds, no empty soil is laid bare to the eye—barren soil being a likely place where some noxious and invasive weed can get its start. Instead, the close quarters allow for interesting combinations of foliage and flowers, layered like a collage. Arching sprays of lady's mantle girdle stiff calendula, shocking magenta rock cress accents a drift of tiny pink-flowered thyme, and umbels of purple fennel stand against variegated ornamental grass.

In this garden, half the plants are free-spirited, blending around nonmotile companions such as peonies, gold-tipped spirea, 'Red Jade' crabapples, and a fringe tree, Thomas Jefferson's favorite tree. Ornamental grasses—glories of the winter garden—sway beside daylilies, with quaking grass often seeding itself. A dwarf Japanese maple assumes a statuesque pose at the end of the lower pond, while blue-flowered creeping veronica and freely seeding lady's mantle spill out beneath it onto the walk. Other creeping perennials making a strong show in the gravel include violets—once candied for Strong's daughter's April birthday—sedums, thymes, lamb's ears,

Veronica creeps out from beneath a dwarf Japanese maple.

103

snow-in-summer, 'Pink Panda' strawberries, and evening prim-roses.

Here and there taller self-seeders like bronze fennel, dame's rocket, calendula, arugula, cilantro, cosmos, spider flow-ers, flowering tobacco, and oxeye daisies emerge in eye-catching flourishes. The original bronze fennel plant was a gift, one that keeps on coming as it now voluntarily self-sows throughout half of the garden. Lemon balm seeds beside a lounge chair where Strong can bask in the sun and inhale its pleasing citrus fragrance.

104

Another gift, a package of love-in-a-mist seeds, has grown into a drift of blue flowers that spread out from a small kitchen garden into nearby gravel.

The garden holds more than mere cultivated plants. The bold upright leaves of burdock, round, horse hoof–shaped leaves of coltsfoot, and rosettes of succulent edible purslane make architectural contribu-tions here and there. The aromatic round leaves and blue flowers of ground ivy cascade over retaining walls and creep beneath trees like a ground cover. Where they complement the overall garden, these wild plants—which a less formidable gardener might call weeds—can stay until they are no longer needed or become overaggressive.

All these free-spirited plants look pleasant and natural—softening and coloring gravel walks without hindering foot traffic. This scheme is not entirely the result of nature's graceful design but relies more on Strong's weeding out any volunteer plants that are awkward or in the way.

Valerie Strong's garden changes to rust and gold in fall as northern sea oats, switch grass, and other perennials prepare for winter dormancy.

Strong says her approach to gardening has changed over the years. She has become satisfied to let the garden break free from the original design and evolve naturally. Instead of trying to control planting arrangements, she prefers to make the most of the plants as they develop. She has been particularly charmed by spontaneous successes such as climbing nasturtium flowers opening in a stiff yew bush to make it resemble a gilded Christmas tree, a bent sunflower blooming at the rim of a birdbath, and a drift of oxeye daisies emerging from a blue sea of veronica. Merely buying plants doesn't mean you own them, Strong believes. They are nature's creatures and should be allowed to procreate and mingle, but with curbing that at times can be ruthless to achieve the visual goals of the designer.

San Francisco Mediterranean Gardens

The idea of planting drought-tolerant natives, Mediterranean plants, and other species from dry climates is catching on in arid parts of the western states, where water supplies are meager and best saved for human activities. The look of a lean, natural California, Texas, Arizona, or other arid climate can be replicated in open landscapes veneered with gravel.

Ideas can be gleaned from the San Francisco–area gardens designed by Ron Lutsko, landscape architect and nature enthusiast, who champions use of native California plants. Because temperatures are warm, summers are dry, and winters can be wet, Lutsko looks for plants that tolerate drought but also withstand occasional winter soakings. These moisture extremes prove to be the biggest challenges to plant survival in this otherwise mild zone 9 and 10 climate.

Lutsko uses gravel gardens to provide sharp drainage for improved winter survival and to echo the dusty aridity of stereotypical Mediterranean areas. He enjoys the simplicity of structure that gravel provides, setting it dramatically apart from lush English gardens, for instance. When combined with free-spirited native plants, his gravel gardens have an open form and lovely naturalistic feel.

Lutsko often includes free-spirited California natives like Matilija poppy (*Romneya coulteri*), with its divided gray-green leaves and large fragrant white flowers during summer. A shrub, it expands by erecting upright shoots, called suckers, from horizontally spreading roots. Another favorite is California fuchsia (*Zauschneria californica* syn. *Epilobium californicum*), a rhizomatous perennial with linear gray leaves and clusters of trumpet-shaped scarlet flowers in late summer and fall.

Some self-seeding plants of preference include satin flower, baby-blue-eyes, California poppy (detailed in the glossary), fragrant Spanish lavender, and tidy tips (*Layia platyglossa*). If you walk beside a California stream or amid her meadows, you might come upon tidy tips, a low-growing annual spreading gray-tinted leaves to the sun and sprouting a flourish of yellow-and-white daisylike flower heads. Should you come upon an older plant with blossoms faded into fruits, you might observe the outer florets maturing into bristly seeds, ready to produce a new generation.

Thwarting Birds

New crops of self-seeding annual flowers can be compromised by birds, who may eat the entire crop at San Francisco's Strybing Arboretum. Birds such as golden-crowned sparrows and California quail are likely to eat and uproot volunteer seedlings of baby-blue-eyes, Chinese snapdragon, and Queen Anne's thimbles. They don't seem to bother California poppies and clarkia, however, and can be kept off other seedlings by covering them with screens.

If your walk takes you out in spring, watch for the purple or pink cup-shaped flowers of satin flower (*Clarkia amoena*), another self-seeding annual well suited to California gardens and gravel. Revealing the plant's true identity, a cross-shaped stigma emerges from the center of the flower and proclaims its membership in the evening primrose family. The flowers and elongated leaves are borne on stems to 2½ feet long,

some standing perkily upright and others riding sprawling stems to the ground.

Using native plants such as tidy tips and satin flower brings the beauty of California wildlands from the fields and meadows into the landscape.

Gravel Guidelines and Horticultural Hints

Building a free-spirited garden, walk, or terrace from gravel is a project that can be accomplished by do-it-yourselfers or professional landscapers. In either case, it's important to know that gravel varies in its horticultural and aesthetic qualities. Rounded pea gravel, which reaches about ¼ inch in diameter, is ideal for free-spirited gravel gardens. Avoid finer crushed stone or gravel with binders, both of which can pack into a firm layer, ideal for walking on but problematic for free-spirited plant growth.

When ordering pea gravel, try to visit the gravel supplier and check out the color and quality of pea gravel before having it delivered. You may be able to choose between white, tan, or light or dark gray pea gravel or even decomposed granite with hints of pink. Always try to get prewashed gravel that is cleaned of river or quarry sediment before it comes to you.

At the simplest, you can make a gravel garden by preparing weed-free soil of good quality and topping it with 2 inches of gravel. For plants that do best with sharp drainage, use 3 or 4 inches of gravel. Plants that need moist growing conditions may prefer a shallower layer of gravel laid over rich, moist soil. As the gravel settles—coming in closer contact with the soil—and accumulates organic matter from fallen leaves, it will suit an even wider range of free-spirited plants. For a more naturalistic look, you can add partly submerged boulders, like stony outcrops, around which free-spirited plants can swirl. To provide for irrigation in dry climates, bury a perforated or soaker hose in the gravel and hook it up to the garden hose when water is needed.

107

Oxeye daisies spread joyously across gravel gardens.

For more heavily tread walks or terraces, you'll find loose gravel is less than ideal because it shifts beneath feet and furniture. Crushed stone will provide a more stable foundation. Begin by excavating about 6 inches deep across the expanse of the walk or terrace. Build a 4-inch-deep, firm foundation of finely crushed stone, compressed mechanically to hard-pack it into place. Sweep a layer of sand into the crushed stone to fill any openings. Build up the edges of the walk with timbers, stone, or brick to keep the gravel from escaping and fill in between with pea gravel. If you decide you want to plant in this walkway, dig down through the foundation, replace it with soil appropriate to the species, and top with gravel.

Gravel gardens and walks are likely to be frequented by self-sowing, free-spirited plants of all kinds. To limit the presence of overaggressive volunteers, deadhead or remove overaggressive seeders before they can strew their seed load. Regularly rake areas you want to keep clear to deter the start of young seedlings. Some gardeners also will use herbicides, including an organic germination inhibitor made of corn gluten, to cut back on excess growth. Of all these options, however, garden designer Valerie Strong recommends hand-weeding, a job that puts the gardener in intimate contact with the garden to experience the plants with sight, sound, scent, and feel.

Dame's rocket, veronica, oxeye daisies, and bearded iris spread beside Valerie Strong's gravel paths.

Glossary of Self-Sowers for Gravel

A great many plants able to tolerate drought or grow in a wide range of well-drained soils can thrive and spread in gravel gardens or beside gravel paths. Here are a few of them, including some special species for warm climates.

CHINESE SNAPDRAGON OR CHINESE HOUSES

(Collinsia bicolor syn. Collinsia heterophylla)

Hardiness: Annual
Exposure: Sun
Some Companions: California poppy, baby-blue-eyes, satin flower
Primary Means of Spreading: Seeds
Aggressiveness: Limited to moderate
Flowering Time: Spring and summer

This native California annual is most likely to perform in a free-spirited fashion in warm climates. Chinese snapdragon, as the name implies, bears clusters of lovely white-and-purple or white-and-pink flowers that resemble snapdragons on stems to 2 feet high. Like snapdragons, they make lasting cut flowers. The leaves are rounded to lance shaped and held in pairs on opposite sides of the stem.

To start Chinese snapdragons, direct-sow seed in spring in cold climates or fall in mild climates. Chinese snapdragons are best grown in a thin layer of gravel over rich garden soil. Plan to irrigate in dry weather. Planting beside more upright plants like yuccas will give Chinese snapdragons support to lean against.

CALIFORNIA POPPIES

(Eschscholzia californica)

Hardiness: Annual
Exposure: Sun
Some Companions: Baby-blue-eyes, satin flower, Chinese snapdragon
Primary Means of Spreading: Seeds
Aggressiveness: Limited to moderate
Flowering Time: Spring, summer, fall, or winter

This may be the most famous native California wildflower and is given credit for this accomplishment by being the official state flower. Once used by Native Americans to treat toothaches, the California poppies are cherished today for naturalistic plantings, flower gardens, rock gardens, and even roadside plantings. Large open-faced flowers of yellow or orange stand to 2 feet high above divided blue-green leaves that are handsome in their own right. Cultivars can sport red, pink, or cream-colored flowers. As the flowers fade, pods develop, containing small, dark, round seeds— much like the poppy seeds found on bagels. If allowed to spill to the earth when mature, they may produce another generation of flowers. In California, peak bloom begins in spring, but flowers can continue to open sporadically through summer and into fall, even winter in warm climates. Deadheading helps extend the flowering season, but diminishes the seed crop. You also can cut flowers while just breaking out of the bud for short-lived flower arrangements.

Start California poppies from seed sown in spring in cool climates, where they may not reseed reliably, or in fall in warm climates. Provide sandy soil or graveled beds over well-drained earth.

INDIAN BLANKET

(Gaillardia pulchella)

Hardiness: Annual
Exposure: Sun
Some Companions: Cockscomb, black-eyed susan, love-lies-bleeding, Jacob's coat
Primary Means of Spreading: Seeds
Aggressiveness: Limited
Flowering Time: Summer and fall

You may be familiar with the widely grown perennial blanket flower (*Gaillardia* x *grandiflora*). Indian blanket is its annual counterpart, an American native that grows wild from Virginia to Florida and west to New Mexico and Colorado. The lanky plants reach 1 to 2 feet high and bear distinctive orange, red, yellow, often bicolor or yellow-tipped daisy-shaped flower heads. The leaves, which lean toward gray green, are elongated or spoon shaped. The flowers, particularly the late-blooming ones, mature into rounded, gray seed heads bearing several dozen hairy nutlets per head. The nutlets may fall near the parent plant and arise next year. In warm climates, they also may be joined by the parent plant, which sometimes survives a mild winter for an encore performance. The flowers make long-lasting bouquets.

Provide sandy soil or graveled beds over well-drained soil. The plant can tolerate salt spray in an ocean-side garden. Deadhead to extend bloom into fall but be certain to allow enough flowers to mature to replenish numbers next year.

BLUE THIMBLE FLOWER OR QUEEN ANNE'S THIMBLES

(Gilia capitata)

Hardiness: Annual
Exposure: Sun
Some Companions: Baby-blue-eyes, satin flower, Chinese snapdragon
Primary Means of Spreading: Seeds

Aggressiveness: Limited to moderate
Flowering Time: Summer to fall

With blue or purple flowers clustered together in a loose head, this native of the western United States most closely resembles an old-fashioned pincushion flower. It is capable of self-sowing in warm climates, but is questionable for cool climates. The plant can reach 2 to 3 feet tall, with finely divided, ferny leaves feathering the base of the plant and stem. While these annuals arise from self-sown or direct-planted seed in spring, they often don't flower until later in the season, providing an extended bloom when grown with early bloomers like California poppies, satin flower, and sweet alyssum.

Provide light sandy soil or a shallow layer of gravel over a garden bed. Blue thimble flowers do best where summers are not too hot and benefit from irrigation during dry weather.

Dame's rocket flowers beside bearded iris and forget-me-nots.

DAME'S ROCKET
(Hesperis matronalis)

Hardiness: Zones 3 to 8
Exposure: Sun to light shade

Some Companions: Garden forget-me-not, sweet alyssum, wild geraniums
Primary Means of Spreading: Seeds
Aggressiveness: Aggressive
Flowering Time: Late spring or early summer

Like the spread of computers across the modern world, sometimes there can be no stopping change. This appears to be the case with dame's rocket. A native of central Europe and southern Asia, it has conquered the rest of Europe and Iceland and also dispersed over much of North America. Many people look forward to seeing the prolific spring show of white, bright purple, or lavender-pink clusters of flowers, which resemble an early-blooming phlox. They are fragrant and can draw butterflies and bees. The elliptical to lance-shaped leaves clothe upright branched stems reaching to 3 feet tall. The flowers mature into silique pods with a row of seeds in each half. They can self-sow abundantly. Some plants behave like biennials, disappearing after setting seeds; still others will come back for another year of bloom.

Provide fertile soil beneath a shallow layer of gravel. Water during dry weather.

OXEYE DAISY
(Leucanthemum vulgare syn. Chrysanthemum leucanthemum)

Hardiness: Zones 3 to 9
Exposure: Sun
Some Companions: Daylilies, sedums, bellflowers, coneflowers, calendula
Primary Means of Spreading: Creeping stems and seeds
Aggressiveness: Aggressive
Flowering Time: Late spring to fall

This early-emerging daisylike flower blooms from late spring into summer or even fall (particularly if deadheaded),

Oxeye daisies are perfectly suited for gravel gardens.

which gives it a very long seed-producing season. It is no surprise that this Eurasian native spreads in bright profusion along many country roads and open fields, and also sneaks into gardens, making itself quite at home in the United States. The short-lived perennial plant grows 1 to 3 feet tall in an upright clump, with inconspicuous toothed leaves forming basal rosettes and climbing up the stem. Short rhizomes can turn one clump into several, but major movement comes from self-sown seeds. The daisylike flowers, with white florets surrounding a golden central disk, are perfect for plucking to determine if "he loves me, he loves me not" or to cut for arrangements. Florets in the central disk switch from male to female, while the outer petal-like florets are solely female, producing seed using pollen from neighboring florets. Each floret develops into one nutlet, which matures about a month after the flower opens.

Provide average soil that is not too fertile, overlaid with a thin layer of gravel. Water during dry weather. Cut back old flowers to prolong bloom but leave enough maturing seeds to ensure a new stand of blooms next year.

111

BUTTER AND EGGS
(Linaria vulgaris)

Hardiness: Zones 4 to 8
Exposure: Sun
Some Companions: Verbascums, verbena, oxeye daisy
Primary Means of Spreading: Creeping stems and seeds
Aggressiveness: Moderate to aggressive
Flowering Time: Summer to fall

This old-fashioned perennial has been mistaken for a native American wildflower. It actually is European but has spread through much of North America, growing in fields, beside roads, in gardens, and also in gravel. The plants conquer new territory in the most free-spirited fashion with creeping runners and self-sown seedlings. Butter and eggs can reach 1 to 3 feet high and has narrow elongated leaves. It is easily identifiable by the snap-dragonlike flowers, usually a two-tone blend of yellow and orange. These flowers, which cannot self-pollinate, attract moths, butterflies, and bees with rich nectar hidden at the base of the flower spur. A pollinator must land on the dark lower lip of the flower, push into the floral throat, and extend a long tongue to the nectar, while rubbing up against the fertile floral organs. Once pollination is accomplished and seed is set, abundant self-seeding is likely to follow.

Provide average garden soil overlaid by a shallow layer of gravel. Divide large clumps and deadhead as needed to control spread.

SWEET ALYSSUM
(Lobularia maritima)

Hardiness: Annual
Exposure: Sun to light shade
Some Companions: Pansies, johnny jump-up, annual lobelia
Primary Means of Spreading: Seeds
Aggressiveness: Limited to moderate
Flowering Time: Spring to fall

This petite annual bears an abundance of small, fragrant, four-petaled flowers of white, purple, or pink on low-growing plants that reach only 4 to 12 inches high. The narrow leaves are nearly hidden when plants are in full bloom. A native of southern Europe, sweet alyssum is commonplace in many American annual gardens and mixed borders. Sweet alyssum also will grow between rock pavers, in rock gardens, or around rock retaining walls. The flowers open in profusion during cool, mild spring weather but often fade out in the heat of summer to return again in fall if deadheaded. In mild climates, they may flower all winter. Allowed to produce seeds, they stretch out valved pods that hold promise for a new generation. Seeds will sprout on the surface of the soil where they fall, as they require light for prompt germination.

Provide fertile soil overlaid by a thin layer of gravel. The initial crop can be planted from seeds or nursery plants in spring or fall. Water during dry weather.

Garden forget-me-not thrives in moist gravel or in rich shade gardens.

GARDEN FORGET-ME-NOT
(Myosotis sylvatica)

Hardiness: Zones 5 to 9
Exposure: Shade
Some Companions: Daffodils, woodland wildflowers, hostas, ferns, Johnny jump-up

Primary Means of Spreading: Seeds
Aggressiveness: Moderate
Flowering Time: Spring to early summer

Once you've grown this lovely plant, it will be hard to forget as it reappears year after year from self-sown seedlings. Sprays of fragrant, yellow-eyed, crystal blue flowers open in abundance in spring, livening up a moist, shady gravel garden, woodland garden, or shady border. Although native to Eurasia, garden forget-me-nots are naturalized in North America. Some self-sown offspring of blue-flowered parents can show up with pink or white flowers. The foliage, which is oval to elongated, stays in the background but can become shabby when seeds are set. The plants can reach to 2 feet tall. Though these plants often behave like biennials, dying back after seeds are set, they may replenish their numbers reliably enough to appear perennial. Their floral fragrance attracts pollinators, which are guided to nectar and pollen by the yellow ring in the center of the flower. If insect pollinators are scarce, flowers can self-pollinate.

Provide average garden soil overlaid with a shallow layer of gravel. Direct-sow seeds or transplant nursery seedlings in spring or fall. Deadhead older flowers to encourage rebloom but leave enough flowers to mature to repopulate the garden next year. Irrigate as needed to keep growing conditions moist during dry weather.

BABY-BLUE-EYES
(Nemophila menziesii)

Hardiness: Annual
Exposure: Sun to light shade
Some Companions: California poppies, satin flower, blue thimble flower, spring bulbs
Primary Means of Spreading: Seeds
Aggressiveness: Limited
Flowering Time: Spring and summer

112

This California native can be a self-sower in mild climates. Reclining stems to 1 foot long have hairy feathered leaves and open-faced light-centered blue flowers. Baby-blue-eyes is a western member of the Virginia waterleaf family, Hydrophyllaceae, and like Virginia waterleaf, it thrives in cool spring weather. Plants are likely to fade when the weather becomes hot, but hopefully not before setting a new crop of seeds.

Provide good garden soil with a shallow surface layer of pea gravel.

Johnny jump-ups can dance from gravel gardens to gardens of roses, perennials, vegetables, and herbs with amazing ease.

JOHNNY JUMP-UP
(*Viola tricolor*)

Hardiness: Zones 4 to 8
Exposure: Sun to light shade
Some Companions: Sweet alyssum, violets, pansies, garden forget-me-not
Primary Means of Spreading: Seeds
Aggressiveness: Moderate to aggressive
Flowering Time: Spring to fall

This charming flower is one of the best representatives of free-spirited flowers. Small plants reaching 6 to 12 inches high have round, scalloped evergreen leaves with pointed tips. The flat-faced flowers have velvety dark purple upper petals, yellow lower petals, and creamy, white, blue, or violet side petals. Darker veins near the floral throat guide insect pollinators to the nectar spur. Abundant seeds are produced, sometimes emerging near the parent plant but often migrating a considerable distance away. Long-blooming Johnny jump-ups can act as annuals, biennials, or perennials. A European native, the plant has become naturalized in North America.

Johnny jump-ups can grow in a wide range of soils, from the rich vegetable garden to the lean rock garden. In the gravel garden, provide average soil with a thin layer of surface gravel. Irrigate during dry weather to prolong bloom and lifetime.

MOSS VERBENA
(*Verbena tenuisecta*)

Hardiness: Zones 8 to 10
Exposure: Sun
Some Companions: Oxeye daisy, 'Flamingo Feather' cockscomb, mother-of-thyme, creeping sedums
Primary Means of Spreading: Creeping stems and seeds
Aggressiveness: Moderate to aggressive
Flowering Time: Summer to fall

Moss verbena is a native of South America that has spread across the southern states. With aromatic leaves on stems that are inclined to creep, it has short spikes of bright lavender, blue, white, or purple flowers. The abundantly produced seeds look like short sections of pencil lead and have self-sown successfully in my zone 5 garden.

A broad range of other verbena species also will self-sow and spread through flower gardens and gravel gardens. Mostly native to the western hemisphere, verbenas are alike in usually having square stems, opposite leaves, and clusters of bright tubular flowers at the top. Especially attractive when growing in abundant colonies, they can cover a garden with blossoms, complementing stay-put perennials and annuals around and amid which they emerge. Verbenas tolerate drought, thrive in gravel, and bloom well through most of the summer.

Tall verbena (*Verbena bonariensis*), named after Buenos Aires, is a native of South America. It is hardy in zones 6 to 9, grows upright to 3 or 4 feet high, and bears bright purple flowers. A successful self-seeder, it has spread into the southern United States.

Rose verbena (*V. canadensis*) is hardy in zones 4 to 10 and grows wild from Mexico and Florida to Colorado and Virginia. It has pink or red flowers and spreading stems 1 to 1 ½ feet long that root where they touch the ground.

Rigid verbena (*V. rigida*) grows upright 1 to 2 feet high and has fragrant purple flowers. Native to South America but naturalized as far north as North Carolina, it is hardy in zones 7 to 10.

MEXICAN ZINNIA
(*Zinnia angustifolia* syn. *Zinnia haageana* or *Zinnia mexicana*)

Hardiness: Annual
Exposure: Sun
Some Companions: Jacob's coat, cockscomb, globe amaranth
Primary Means of Spreading: Seeds
Aggressiveness: Limited to moderate
Flowering Time: Summer and fall

In warm climates, this festive-flowered native Mexican annual can be likely to self-sow. Growing upright, reaching 15 to 24 inches high, and bearing oblong to linear hairy leaves, Mexican zinnias are topped by bright daisylike orange flowers. Some forms are marked with yellow or red. Flower heads mature into an abundance of seeds, as dozens of individual flowers, called florets, make up each head.

Provide ordinary garden soil overlaid with a shallow layer of gravel. Water during dry weather.

Freely seeding vining
petunias grow beside
heirloom crops at Seed
Savers Exchange.

CHAPTER 7:
creative kitchen gardens

Why not have a free-spirited garden and eat it too? A variety of delicious old-fashioned and new crops may arise from self-sown seeds or spread on runners or horizontal roots. These gifts of nature usually fulfill their potential best if transplanted into regularly spaced rows and wide beds that ensure each plant has enough soil, sun, and space to thrive. As a result, the free-spirited kitchen garden often assumes the form of an organized working garden, but consists of at least some vegetables, berries, and edible flowers that have arrived on their own.

Arugula, an aromatic salad green with undertones of mustard-garlic, swells into a succulent rosette of lobed leaves in

Arugula, identifiable by its tall lobed leaves, grows amid lettuce, chervil, and other greens in the author's garden.

spring, stretches up white flowers in early summer, drops small dark seeds, and returns from self-sown seeds again in late summer, fall, or spring. Mustard, with tasty seeds and spicy young salad greens, produces enough long-lived seeds to pepper a portion of the garden now and for several years to come.

A fallen cherry tomato, rotting in rich soil to set seeds free on the earth, can sprout into a clump of little tomato plants during the warmth of late summer. Some still-dormant seeds may survive winter temperatures that would kill the parent plant, to emerge when summer heat arrives next year. Tomatillos, mild-flavored tomato relatives that make wonderful salsas, may start so easily from self-sown seeds that they never need replanting. In a compost pile, where old innards of a 'Blue Hubbard' squash were dumped, a vigorously growing new vine may sprout, nourished by the nutrient soup of decaying leaves and grass clippings.

Because they mature quickly, annual vegetables tend to be good candidates for self-seeding. Some modern annual seed crops like beans, peas, and corn, however, have been bred to hold their seeds within tightly sealed pods or ears for easy harvest, which can limit self-seeding potential. But more primitive seed crops like sunflowers and grain amaranth or vegetables grown for their succulent leaves and roots like salad burnet, sorrel, and Chinese spinach, freely shed their seeds when ripe, a natural adaption that ensures proliferation of new generations.

Self-seeding becomes more complicated with biennial crops such as cabbage, cauliflower, brussels sprouts, carrots, and beets. These vegetables won't flower and produce seeds until the second year of life. The first year is devoted to growing large, leafy plants and big succulent heads, best done without the energy drain of flower and seed production. But to complete a seed cycle, plants must survive winter, an often questionable proposition in cold climates.

To rely on self-seeders alone would be a mistake. A few perennial garden crops, such as Jerusalem artichokes, horseradish, and garden sorrel, spread with underground stems and roots. Horseradish has rapidly expanding clumps of deep pungent roots. Jerusalem artichokes have wide spreading roots, each of which yield crunchy tubers capable of sprouting into a new plant if left unharvested. Raspberries and blackberries, spreading on roots or rooted stems, also display aggressive vigor and movement.

Self-seeding purple coneflowers and spider flowers stand in decorative gardens near productive vegetable fields.

117

All told, there are plenty of free foods just waiting for a chance to be turned loose in a garden. Sample one, several, or many free-spirited vegetables, edible flowers, and berries for culinary abundance like you've never experienced before.

Seed Savers Exchange, Where Self-Seeding Is Applauded

Diane and Kent Whealy of the Seed Savers Exchange, a nonprofit organization devoted to preserving old-fashioned and open-pollinated seeds, appreciate self-seeding ability in certain crops. Having collected heirloom and endangered vegetables from across the world, the Whealys

Why Open-Pollinated Vegetables?

When you allow crops to self-sow and want the second generation to be as good as the first, you should start with open-pollinated vegetables. They can freely interbreed with others of the same variety or cultivar and come true, fulfilling the standards expected of that particular type of plant.

Hybrid seed, in contrast, is the product of cross-pollination between compatible varieties intentionally crossed by seed companies or inadvertently crossed in the garden. The hybrid offspring have characteristics of both parents in a unique blend all their own. If you like sweet bell peppers but grow one beside a hot chili pepper and allow the two to interbreed, their offspring may produce fruits varying from mild to hot. The problem is you won't know what to expect until you bite into one. That hybrid no longer can be called by either parent's name and does not maintain the purity of either original variety.

Intentional hybridization by seed companies has been used to produce high-performance hybrids well loved by modern gardeners. As when breeding champion racehorses, plant breeders keep careful track of the ancestry of each cross. They gradually mold new generations by choosing parentage that will endow special characteristics—earlier production, brighter colors, sweeter flavor, or disease resistance. If these hybrids are allowed to go to seed, however, their offspring have varying genetics and a potpourri of characteristics, often quite unlike the mother plant.

grow a sampling each year. These crops are allowed to mature beyond peak harvest time, a requirement for setting seed that can be saved for future generations. As they harvest and clean cherished seeds out in rich farm fields and attractive demonstration gardens, some seeds escape and show their ability to return independently.

Located in Decorah, Iowa, the Whealy's Heritage Farm experiences intense winter cold—temperatures that drop to -30 ° F. Even so, a variety of vegetable seeds survive winter to grow in spring or summer.

Lettuce is one crop that often returns from seed. When tender leafy heads mature, they fill with bitter milky sap and erect a tall flowering stem, a time when they are usually removed from the vegetable garden. But if you allow them to flower and go to seed, you can enjoy the benefit of free-spirited offspring. The young self-sown lettuces will only come true if you don't grow two varieties side by side. But it's hard to go wrong with lettuce, and even cross-pollinated seedlings usually are delightful.

Tomatoes, beans freed from their pods, and even potato tubers missed during summer harvests will return in spring to gamely put in a second year of growth. Peas raised in spring for a summer harvest often are inclined to reseed again for a fall crop.

A top priority at the Seed Savers Exchange is maintaining the purity of each seed strain. Measures are always taken to prevent outcrossing that would contaminate and change varieties they are working to save. Peppers, for instance, are grown in screened cages covered with fine mesh to keep out sweat bees and other pollinators carrying foreign pollen.

With sunflowers, only one cultivar is grown each year so no errant pollen will be available to adulterate the seed produced. Because birds love sunflower seeds and will eat every last one when the heads turn yellow,

'Rustov' Russian sunflowers are protected under bird netting.

rows of plants are covered with mesh netting that stretches down to the ground and keeps them safe from hungry beaks. Diane Whealy harvests the seeds before the heads dry out enough to allow the seeds to drop to the ground, although inevitably some do fall free and arise the following year. They are conscientiously uprooted, however, to prevent interbreeding with the special sunflower variety of the new year.

Squash may self-sow if a mature winter squash or pumpkin is left outside by mistake. Volunteer squash seedlings, which might be fun to let

Grandpa Ott's Morning Glory

At Heritage Farm, a garden entryway arbor and one side of a 40-foot-tall red barn are covered with Grandpa Ott's morning glory. This vigorous self-seeder, with irridescent purple flowers and red throats, is responsible for the birth of the Seed Savers Exchange.

It all began when Diane Whealy's great-grandfather brought this particular morning glory from Bavaria to the United States and passed the seeds along to his son, Whealy's Grandpa Ott. He and his grandchildren spent languid summer days playing on a porch screened by this productive vine. It was given twine to climb and formed a solid wall of greenery broken only by a whimsical window opening, with a shape that varied each year.

Of Grandpa Ott's nine children and over fifty grandchildren, Whealy was the only one to ask for the morning glory seeds and continue growing it after he passed away. If she had not taken it under her wing, this plant could have been lost. This realization, and the recognition that other heirloom plants are disappearing all over the country, inspired Whealy and her husband to head up Seed Savers Exchange. As of 1997, they had saved eighteen thousand varieties of vegetables and seven-hundred nineteenth century apples.

Grandpa Ott's morning glory.

grow in an ordinary home garden, are routed out of Heritage Farm fields to avoid cross-pollination.

Marvelous, juicy June-bearing 'North Sea' strawberries have multiplied from three small plants to a large 15-foot-square patch. Their success comes not from self-sowing but from stretching out white-stemmed runners that sprout new plantlets at the end.

Vegetables and berries are not the only free-spirited plants to be found at Heritage Farm. In the display gardens, enclosed by picturesque white rail fences and backed up to a huge red barn, dancing colors of self-sown annual flowers

spread amid the placid greenery of ripening vegetables. Beneath some of the trellised beans and amid maturing onions are old-fashioned vining petunias, with evening-fragrant, mellow pink, lavender, purple, and white flowers on lanky semierect stems 1½ to 2 feet long. Their tiny seeds have spread to every display garden from a small planting made four years ago. Although most seedlings are weeded out, some are left here and there for their carefree color.

Vining petunias grow beside Swiss chard and onions.

Flowering tobaccos—pink or red-flowered *Nicotiana alata* and white-flowered *N. sylvestris*—reseed abundantly around a network of pepper isolation cages in seed production fields. The tiny flowering tobacco seeds were left behind after the flowers were grown there the previous year and have colonized every square inch of space. The volunteer seedlings emerged, somewhat surprisingly, in midsummer when the ground was thoroughly warm. They burst into bloom a month later, their productivity outshining transplants set out in a display garden earlier in the year.

The blend of flowers and vegetables at Heritage Farm is both beautiful and productive, an ideal example of free-spirited garden potential.

Greens and Grains of the Southwest

In addition to tender leafy greens like lettuce and spinach or classic grains like corn and wheat, you can grow delightful, freely seeding species from the American Southwest and Mexico. They include amaranths, chenopods, and mustards—cultivated edible-leaved relatives of common weeds with the ability to grow in tough situations. They produce seeds in abundance, emerging around parent plants or spreading in tilled soil to clothe freshly worked ground. Many seeds remain viable for extended periods and may sprout for several seasons to come—a blessing or a curse.

Originally harvested from the wild by hunting and gathering tribes, these crops have easy-growing tendencies and an ability to colonize any open ground, making them naturals for earliest agriculture. Many have remained in gardens of Native Americans and other people who cling to traditional ways and are being safeguarded and sold by Native Seeds/SEARCH, a Tucson-based preservation organization.

Chual and several other forms of *Chenopodium berlandieri* hail from Mexico and are harvested for their nutrient-rich young leaves or developing seed stalks, which are popular cooked with eggs and cheese. Should these chenopods begin a greedy takeover plan, cut or pull excess young seedlings for delightful salads of mixed baby greens.

Orach or wild spinach (*Atriplex hortensis*), a close relative of *Chenopodium*, is ideal for difficult climates from northern Mexico to the northern plains. The young leaves are eaten like spinach, but have a slight salty flavor, and the seeds, which are rich in vitamin A, can be ground into flour. When mature, plants can reach 8 feet tall, with tiny flowers packed into terminal spikes that may reach over a foot long. Delaying flowering by keeping plants moist and well fertilized helps provide an extended leaf harvest. Red- and yellow-leaved forms of orach also may be found in the ornamental garden, where their attractive foliage looks great amid annual and perennial flowers.

No discussion of aggressive seeders would be complete without mentioning mustards. Although most mustards hail from the Old World, they have become widespread weeds throughout North America. Rape seed oil, mustard powder, stadium mustard, and more products are made from abundantly yielded mustard seeds. The spicy leaves, called mustard greens, are also harvested from a number of mustard species (see page 129). Mostaza Roja with large, red-veined leaves is a Hispanic heirloom variety from northeast New Mexico. Tarahumara Mostaza is a wild mustard eaten fresh in salads, boiled, or steamed.

Grain amaranth (*Amaranthus cruentus*), grown in Mexico and the Southwest for centuries, is a high-performance crop that needs about 140

Left, Squash flowers require insects for cross-pollination and require special care to preserve seed purity. Below, this year's forgotten potato tubers may resprout into flourishing plants next year.

123

frost-free days to bring its ripe seed to matura-tion. A staple of ancient Aztec and Mayan civi-lizations, ama-ranth cultivation was forbidden by conquering Spanish rulers in the 1500s. But the plant and its many varieties continued to grow wild and so are still available today. The high-protein seeds are borne on long colorful fronds made up of tiny, thickly clustered fruits. 'Alegria' has blond seed that is popped and mixed with honey in central Mexico. Hopi red dye (*A. cruentus* 'Komo') has scarlet flower bracts used to make natural food dye. Other amaranth seeds are ground for flour or cooked whole for cereal. You also can harvest the young leaves for salads or cooked vegetables. If you like the taste, consider planting leaf amaranth (see page 129).

'Spookie' pumpkins are a type of win-ter squash.

Cole Crops in the Pacific Northwest

Biennial crops, which require a cold winter dormant period before they can flower and set seed, usually are not hardy enough to sur-vive northern winters without protection. But some of the hardiest cole crops—kale, brussels sprouts, and winter cabbages, in particular—sail through winters in the Pacific Northwest, where temperatures seldom drop below 15° F. Some can seed successfully enough to be free-spirited. The best survivors ordinarily come from sturdy northern European stock, varieties bred to be harvested during fall and winter.

The beauty of allowing biennial kale, cabbage, and brussels

sprouts to self-sow is the perfect sequence of events. Seeds dropped in summer naturally arise just in time to produce a new crop for harvest in fall, winter, or spring. If you don't harvest every plant and allow a few to overwinter and seed, the cycle will begin again.

In Cottage Grove, Oregon, the open-pollinated seed production fields of the Territorial Seed Company sometimes are enriched with self-sowing cole crops. The volunteer seedlings are generated from seeds dropped during seed harvest and cleaning, and can be identified from the planted crop by their tendency to grow between the rows.

The most outstanding self-sower is 'Winter Red' kale, which produces magnificent volunteer stands each year. 'Winter Red' has slightly frilled, oak-shaped leaves that turn red and violet in fall. The fresh, young leaves grow sweeter when exposed to frost. In spring, upright 5-foot-tall stalks arise, bearing small yellow flowers followed by seeds, which complete the plant's life cycle before it dies.

'Red Rubine' is one of the hardiest open-pollinated brussels sprout cultivars and may survive winter where temperatures get no lower than 10° F. If allowed to flower in spring and set seeds, it is a good candidate for seed production.

Winter cabbages bred for planting in summer, wintering in the garden, and harvesting in spring are another self-seeding possibility. 'January King', a beautiful, ruby-tinted, open-pollinated cabbage, has survived freezing solid and temperatures of 7° F without damage. If left unharvested until spring, the flower stalk will push up through the head, a process you can assist by slicing the head shallowly. The full-sized flower stalk reaches several feet high to produce airy clusters of yellow flowers and their all-important seeds.

In areas like Decorah, Iowa, where winters are colder than 10 to 20° F, dedicated seed collectors bring potted plants into a cool root cellar in fall and replant them outdoors in early spring. They also take precautions because all of these cole crops can interbreed. Enclosing plants in screened cages prevents random pollination and maintains variety purity.

Horticultural Hints

Easy-care gardeners choose free-spirited flowers that will grow best in the existing soil and site. When it comes to growing food crops, most people choose vegetables, herbs, and berries based on their flavor. You may need to improve the garden soil, find a suitably sunny location and, perhaps, water and fertilize extra to upgrade the growing conditions for great results. Your initial effort will be justly rewarded later when you can pick succulent, sweet, tender leaves, fruits, or roots.

Vegetables such as cabbages, broccoli, kale, peppers, eggplant, tomatoes, lettuce, and spinach are a greedy lot, preferring rich, moist, fertile soil. You can convert almost any soil into their favored playground by adding extra compost—by the truckload for poor soils or by the wheelbarrow load for average soils. Building raised beds or planting in raised mounds of good soil increases soil depth and improves water drainage, easy ways to make marginal conditions better.

Crops capable of self-seeding in your area will only be able to do so if harvested lightly enough to allow them to go to seed. Warm-climate gardeners growing kale, for instance, could remove a few leaves from a strapping young plant but should avoid stripping away any more or the plant may not survive winter or have the strength to flower. Likewise, a head of lettuce, cut free at the base, leaves only a shell of a plant unlikely to muster the strength to flower.

After flowering, the seeds must mature until the embryos are well formed, the food reserves stored, and the seed coats hardened protectively. Plants like radishes and arugula develop dry, dark pods that will break open to spill the mature seeds. With fleshy, succulent tomatoes, however, the soft fruit turns sweet and bright red as the seeds mature but must rot to release the seeds. Hard-shelled fruits like squash or gourds may not rot fast enough to release the viable seeds and may need to be broken open to yield volunteer offspring next year.

After seeds have been cast, you need to know what the seedlings look like so you do not obliterate them with hoe or tiller. Most seedlings first send up a cotyledon, a leaf often shaped similarly to the seed with little to no resemblance to the true leaves that will soon follow. Once past the cotyledon stage, little lettuce seedlings are easily identified by their broad, light green to red leaves, miniature replicas of parent plants. Seedling tomatoes, likewise, bear distinctive divided leaves. Nearly wild greens such as amaranth, however, can be quite difficult to tell from their weedy cousins and should be studied when first planted to help distinguish the better seedlings later on.

Close-packed clusters of self-sown seedlings, squeezed for space, sun, nutrients, and moisture, often struggle and fizzle out before harvest time. You can save them from their own overcrowding by transplanting volunteer seedlings when they are small and have one or several sets of true leaves. Spread seedlings out along a single row or, to save space, give them each a square of open space in a 2- or 3-foot-wide bed. Leaf lettuce grows nicely in a 6- to 8-inch-square opening while tomatillos need more space, a 2-foot-square opening.

When you consider the growth habits of different crops, you may find two that can share the same space. Quick-maturing greens like mustard and arugula, sprouting voluntarily in spring and cut for the salad bowl by early summer, will leave space for beans, squash, or other warm-season vegetables to spread out later on. As self-sown seeds arise when the

Sweet cherry tomatoes, mild, fuzzy-skinned yellow 'Garden Peach' tomatoes, and great-flavored 'Brandywine' tomatoes all will self-sow.

temperature best suits them, a free-spirited kitchen garden can make maximum use of changing seasons.

Isolation Cages

If you become serious about maintaining the purity of seeds, you may want to add a couple isolation cages to the garden. Isolation cages are rectangular wooden frames, reaching about 3 feet high and 4 to 6 feet long, and covered with fine screening that will keep out free-flying pollinating insects. For crops such as squash that need cross-pollination, you can introduce captive bees and other pollinators inside the cage to spread pollen or do it yourself with a small paintbrush. Crops like tomatoes and peppers will self-pollinate, needing no further effort. You can save the seeds for future use or allow self-sown seedlings to emerge and move them into the main garden.

128

Flowering tobacco clusters around pepper isolation cages at Seed Savers Exchange.

Glossary of Self-Sowing and Creeping Edibles

Many garden vegetables are annuals that spread by seeds, while some perennial crops have creeping roots or spreading tubers that advance to conquer more territory year after year and beg for a heavy harvest to thin them out.

CHINESE SPINACH OR TAMPALA

(Amaranthus tricolor)

Hardiness: Annual
Exposure: Sun
Some Companions: Mustard, arugula, pot marigold
Primary Means of Spreading: Seeds
Aggressiveness: Moderate to aggressive
Flowering Time: Summer or fall

This species of amaranth includes edible forms and ornamentals with multicolored leaves like volcanic 'Molten Fire' with scarlet-centered maroon leaves and 'Joseph's Coat' with crimson, gold, chocolate, and green leaves. The edible forms, often cultivated in Asia, have been selected for their tasty, tender leaves. Fresh leaves are especially high in protein, calcium, and iron but also harbor oxalates and nitrates and should be consumed in moderation. The bushy plants are covered with mostly oval leaves and summer spires of tiny flowers that can reach over 4 feet high. Chinese spinach and other amaranths have an especially efficient metabolism that allows for peak performance in warm, sunny settings—areas with hot summers or tropical heat. Amaranths are wind pollinated, bearing large quantities of lightweight pollen that is tossed in the wind from one plant to the next. Different varieties of *Amaranthus tricolor* can interbreed, blending characteristics for better or worse, but they cannot breed with other species—weeds and grain amaranths. To maintain purity of a given variety, plant only one type each year.

You can start a Chinese spinach bed by strewing seeds across finely tilled earth and covering them very lightly with soil. The tiny seedlings are sensitive to dry soils, but once plants get larger they can tolerate drought. Thin or transplant seedlings to stand 4 to 6 inches apart.

HORSERADISH

(Armoracia rusticana)

Hardiness: Zones 3 to 8
Exposure: Sun
Some Companions: Jerusalem artichoke, asparagus
Primary Means of Spreading: Roots
Aggressiveness: Moderate to aggressive

This old-fashioned perennial straddles the line between vegetable, herb, and spice and adds character to a kitchen garden. Large, coarse leaves emerge directly from the ground, waving elongated blades up to 3 feet high. They grow in thick clumps with ever-expanding waistlines. The pungent roots below ground can reach several feet deep, with long, fleshy, carrotlike roots and clusters of smaller side roots branching off and around them. Although horseradish may occasionally flower, it doesn't set seed. Native to southeastern Europe, horseradish has been grown in the United States since early colonial times and in many places has escaped and naturalized. In fall, when the leaves go dormant, you can dig up larger roots for making roast beef sauces and Bloody Marys, and reset the smaller side roots for next season. Even if you forget to replant, horseradish is likely to come back from deeply buried roots or unharvested side sprouts mistakenly left behind.

Provide rich, moist soil for rapid spread, although horseradish also can grow in less fertile soils.

CHINESE MUSTARD OR GAI CHOI

(Brassica hirta)

Hardiness: Annual
Exposure: Sun
Some Companions: Arugula, lettuce, spinach
Primary Means of Spreading: Seeds
Aggressiveness: Moderate to aggressive
Flowering Time: Summer

Of the many mustard species available, Chinese mustard, native to Russia and Central Asia and naturalized in North America, may be the most useful in the home garden. It is grown for the big, flavorful, lobed or divided leaves, which can reach 10 inches long. When provided with cool, moist conditions, they have a delicious, mild spiciness that tastes great when mixed with milder greens like lettuce or spinach. There are a number of varieties of mustard greens, some with finely cut curly-edged leaves and others with extra-broad leaves. Because various varieties can interbreed, grow only one variety if you want to maintain the purity of its seed. When plants mature or the weather gets warm, they bolt to flower, sending up lanky 4-foot-tall stalks with bright yellow flowers that rely on insects for pollination.

Provide rich, moist soil for best results. Thin or transplant seedlings to stand about 6 inches apart.

POT MARIGOLD

(Calendula officinalis)

Hardiness: Annual
Exposure: Sun

Pot marigolds emerge beside lamb's ears.

Some Companions: Pansy, sweet
alyssum, cabbage, kale
Primary Means of Spreading: Seeds
Aggressiveness: Limited to moderate
Flowering Time: Spring, summer, or fall

130

This many-talented plant, which reaches to
2 feet tall, is useful as a cut flower and an
edible flower. The daisy-shaped yellow,
orange, or cream-colored blossoms have a
mild bitter flavor that is interesting in
small amounts. Once used as a substitute
for saffron, the finely chopped, brightly
colored petals will turn sauces golden
orange. They also are added to teas and salads, and floated on soups, as much for their
bold colors as for their flavor. Romans
spread the joys of calendulas, natives of
Eurasia, across Europe to England, and
from there settlers brought it to North
America. Although the flowers resemble
marigolds, the elongated leaves proclaim
otherwise. Unlike marigolds, calendulas
prefer cool weather. If planted in mild
spring weather, they may thrive until the
heat of summer, scattering seeds as the
flowers mature. New seedlings may arise in
late summer or fall, when temperatures
grow cool again. For a long period of bloom,
remove faded flower heads, but for free-

spirited returns, leave at least a few flowers
to mature and spill their seeds, boat-
shaped achenes. Volunteer seedlings often
have single flowers and seldom grow into
fluffy-headed double forms.

Provide moist but well-drained soil,
and thin or transplant young seedlings to
stand about 1 foot apart.

SQUASH
(Cucurbita spp.)

Hardiness: Annual
Exposure: Sun
Some Companions: Bean, corn,
sunflowers
Primary Means of Spreading: Seeds
Aggressiveness: Limited
Flowering Time: Summer

Squash have been bred for centuries, first
by Native Americans of North and South
America, and more recently and quite
intensively by commercial plant breeders,
producing an intriguing variety available
for gardeners. In the kitchen, there are two
different kinds of squash—hard-shelled
winter keepers like butternut squash,
pumpkins, and hubbard squash, all of
which are allowed to mature in the garden
and produce ripe seeds. Summer squash
like zucchini and crookneck squash are
eaten tender and young and so are less
likely to bear mature seeds that can self-
sow. Botanically, most squash belong to
one of four different species, each abound-
ing with varieties that will interbreed with
others of the same species. If you are con-
cerned about maintaining purity of varieties, plant one variety from each
species to prevent outcrossing and keep
seedling offspring true to its ancestry.

Cucurbita maxima, which includes
banana, buttercup, hubbard, turban winter
squash, and some pumpkins, have long
rambling vines and huge hairy leaves.

C. pepo, including popular acorn, crookneck, scallop, spaghetti squash, zucchini,
and some pumpkins, are characterized by
prickly leaves and five angled sides on the
fruit stem. *C. moschata*, including butternut, cheese, crookneck, and golden cushaw
squash, and some pumpkins, are similarly
large and flamboyant, with dark green
leaves and a flaring fruit stem. *C. mixta*
(syn. *C. argyrosperma*), which produces
green-striped and white cushaw squash,
looks similar but has lighter leaves and
minimal fruit-stem flaring.

Provide rich, moist soil mounded into
raised hills enriched with extra compost or
composed livestock manure. Because the
roots are brittle and easily damaged, move
self-sown seedlings carefully. Scoop up the
soil encased roots with a shovel and replant
without breaking up the protective soil-
encased root ball.

ARUGULA OR ROQUETTE
(Eruca sativa)

Hardiness: Annual
Exposure: Sun
Some Companions: Mustard, lettuce,
spinach
Primary Means of Spreading: Seeds
Aggressiveness: Moderate
Flowering Time: Late spring, summer,
or fall

Arugula, a Mediterranean vegetable
beloved by ancient Romans, also makes a
fine free-spirited offering for contemporary American gardens. The pungent mustard-garlic flavor of arugula is featured in
some gourmet restaurant salads. What only
a gardener would know is how easy and
inexpensively you can grow arugula.
Planted in a cool growing season, seeds
quickly sprout into a rosette of dark green,
lobed leaves 4 to 10 inches long, the size
often correlated to increasing soil fertility

and moisture. When plants mature or the weather becomes warm, arugula plants send up a tall stalk with four-petaled yellow-white blossoms that require insect pollination to be fruitful. Allowed to mature fully, seed capsules will spill ripe seed to the ground, preparing for another generation. Arugula seeds, however, must be fully mature to be viable.

Provide moist, rich soil with good fertility and a high organic content. Arugula also will grow on less desirable soils but not as lushly. Thin seedlings to 6 inches apart. If flea beetles threaten to riddle the leaves with holes, cover plantings with floating row covers, lightweight fabrics that let air, sun, and rain in but keep out flying insects.

STRAWBERRY

(Fragaria x ananassa and Fragaria vesca)

Hardiness: Zones 3 to 10
Exposure: Sun
Some Companions: Fruit trees, fruit bushes, rhubarb, asparagus
Primary Means of Spreading: Creeping stems for traditional strawberries and seeds for alpine strawberries
Aggressiveness: Moderate to aggressive
Flowering Time: Spring or summer

Traditional garden strawberries, with handsome 3-parted compound leaves and a spiderweb of creeping white runners that sprout into new plantlets, make attractive and productive ground covers. Open-faced white blossoms, with a bushy circle of stamens inside, require insect pollination to mature into plump berries. Berries, although they appear solid, are aggregates of many tiny fruits, each of which develops around a miniature black seed. The seed serves primarily to encourage berry development. June-bearing strawberries flower in spring and produce their entire crop in June. They tend to be vigorous spreaders, producing abundant runners and quickly colonizing new territory. Day-neutral strawberries bear flowers and fruits most of the growing season, except during very hot weather. Unlike June bearing types, day-neutral seldom send out many runners.

Alpine strawberries (*Fragaria vesca*) have smaller, slightly less sweet but intensely flavorful berries produced by self-pollinating flowers. They begin ripening in late spring or early summer and continue into fall. The plants lack runners but can produce a bevy of seedlings from unharvested berries. Seedlings may arise not only around the parent plants but also between patio stones or in gravel gardens.

Provide all strawberries with rich, moist but well-drained soil. For best productivity, you can thin dense colonies of June-bearing strawberries so each plant has a square foot of growing space. Alpine strawberries can grow as close as 8 inches apart. If frost threatens early blooms of June bearers, cover plantings with a floating row cover or nighttime blanket for protection.

SUNFLOWERS

(Helianthus annuus)

Hardiness: Annual
Exposure: Sun
Some Companions: Corn, bean, squash
Primary Means of Spreading: Seeds
Aggressiveness: Moderate
Flowering Time: Summer or fall

Sunflowers grow 5 to 10 feet tall, with broad, triangular, roughly hairy leaves along an upright stem and one or several flower heads at the summit. The original species has a central, inch-wide, red-brown seed-bearing disk and a fringe of yellow florets around the outside. Contemporary cultivars can have a seed-bearing disk up to a foot across. Varieties bred for big country bouquets have branched stems and smaller flowers. All these different varieties of *Helianthus annuus* can interbreed if you plant more than one variety each year. With flowers said to follow the path of the sun as it moves through the sky during the day, sunflowers were a sacred symbol to some Mexican and South American cultures. Early American settlers caught sunflower fever and carried its oil-rich seeds across the country, allowing its escape to meadows and disturbed places. Today it can be seen growing in cracks in the pavement beside the Tri-State Freeway around Chicago.

Provide well-drained soil of average fertility, thinning seedlings to about 18 inches apart. The plants quickly stretch up tall, bloom briefly, then grow heavy with seeds. Cover the developing heads with a paper bag, tied to the stem below the head, or cover plants with bird netting to keep sparrows and goldfinches from pecking the seeds out.

JERUSALEM ARTICHOKE

(Helianthus tuberosus)

Hardiness: Zones 2 to 9
Exposure: Sun
Some Companions: Horseradish
Primary Means of Spreading: Tuberous roots
Aggressiveness: Aggressive
Flowering Time: Late summer or fall

Jerusalem artichokes, also called sunchokes or sunroots, are big and bold. Strong stalks rise 8 to 12 feet high with oval hairy leaves to 1 foot long. Some varieties produce clusters of modest, yellow daisy-like flowers. Notorious for spreading rambunctiously, each plant can develop a handful to more than a dozen tubers, each capable of developing into one or several new plants. This inevitably means a big harvest, gathered in fall after frost. The tubers, which can be knobby, round, or elongated with brown, red, or gold skins, taste like water chestnuts and are best cooked lightly, if at all. Indigenous to the eastern United States, Jerusalem artichokes were first cultivated by Native Americans. Early colonists learned to rely on the crisp, mild-flavored tuberous roots for winter staples. When introduced to Europe early in the seventeenth century, the knobby tubers quickly changed from a novelty to commonplace. Use diminished with the arrival of the potato, a larger tuber that was easier to handle in the kitchen. The odd and misleading name, Jerusalem artichoke, is a derivation of Italian *girasole articocco* meaning "sunflower artichoke."

Plant Jerusalem artichokes in any well-drained soil, preferably somewhere separate from the rest of the garden so they can't overwhelm other crops.

132

TOMATOES

(*Lycopersicon esculentum*)

Hardiness: Annual
Exposure: Sun
Some Companions: Peppers, eggplant, basil, sweet marjoram
Primary Means of Spreading: Seeds
Aggressiveness: Limited to moderate
Flowering Time: Summer and fall

Tomatoes, native to South and Central America, were taken back to Spain by Christopher Columbus. Because they belong to the poisonous nightshade family, the thought of eating tomatoes was viewed with suspicion. Italy and Spain, in the mid 1500s, were among the first European countries to give it a try. It was three hundred years later that tomatoes were accepted into colonial American cuisine. In a complete turnaround, today they are revered as a source of vitamin C, vitamin A, and other healthy nutrients. Once tomatoes were established in American gardens, a diversity of varieties developed—a rainbow of colors, from green, grapelike fruit to pale white, yellow, orange, pink, and

purple. Now called heirlooms, these early tomatoes tend to be open pollinated and suitable for free-spirited self-sowing. Many modern varieties are hybrids, not likely to come true from self-sown seeds. Tomatoes usually self-pollinate, needing no isolation or caging to maintain variety purity. The juicy pulp of the tomato, a berry, contains germination inhibitors that prevent seeds from sprouting while held inside. But when an old tomato is tossed on the compost pile or escapes fall garden cleanup, it rots away and leaves the seeds free to germinate when conditions are right.

Plant in rich, moist but well-drained soil. Transplant seedlings 2 ½ to 3 feet apart. It's best to put them in a location where tomatoes and related tomatillos, peppers, and eggplants haven't grown recently to minimize the buildup of problems. Cage young tomatoes so the lanky vines will grow neatly up instead of sprawling out. Mulch with compost to help keep the soil evenly moist and fertile without being excessively high in nitrogen.

Scarlet runner beans grow on a teepee of poles at Seed Savers Exchange.

SCARLET RUNNER BEANS

(*Phaseolus coccineus*)

Hardiness: Zone 10 or annual
Exposure: Sun
Some Companions: Hyacinth pea, squash, corn, sunflowers, climbing nasturtium
Primary Means of Spreading: Seeds
Aggressiveness: Limited
Flowering Time: Summer and fall

Scarlet runner bean is a vining legume with edible 1-foot long bean pods and brilliant scarlet pea-shaped flowers attractive to hummingbirds. The vine, which can reach 10 feet long, has glossy, oval, three-parted leaflets. Originating in tropical America, it was sent to Europe by curious European explorers. From Europe it returned to the Western Hemisphere with settlers. Insect or hummingbird pollination is required for bean production and can result in hybridization between different varieties, including white-flowered Dutch runner (*Phaseolus coccineus 'Albus'*). To allow self-sowing, permit the beans to mature and dry on the vine, spilling some ripe seed to the soil.

Provide loose, light soil and a post, fence, trellis, or arbor for runner beans to twine up. In hot climates, runner beans are perennial, forming an inedible tuberous root that sprouts new vines in spring warmth.

TOMATILLOS

(*Physalis ixocarpa*)

Hardiness: Zone 8 to 10 or annual
Exposure: Sun
Some Companions: Tomatoes, peppers, eggplant
Primary Means of Spreading: Seeds
Aggressiveness: Limited
Flowering Time: Summer and fall

Like its cousin, the tomato, tomatillos are tender perennials with moderately hardy seeds that may produce free-spirited crops year after year. Native to Mexico and naturalized in the eastern United States, it is well loved in Mexican and southwestern cuisine. The elongated to oval leaves arise on floppy stems that can reach 5 feet. Small yellow-and-purple flowers develop into green, gold, or purple berries, which look much like little tomatoes but are wrapped in a papery husk. The berries have a rich, mild flavor and are excellent in salsas. Because tomatillo flowers are self-pollinating, seed purity is easily maintained, particularly if you grow only one variety of this species. Excess fruit must be allowed to mature fully and fall to the ground to permit self-seeding.

Provide rich, moist fertile soil without excessive nitrogen. Transplant clustered seedlings to about 2 feet apart, preferably moving them to a site where tomatillos, tomatoes, peppers, and related plants haven't grown recently. Cage young plants in commercial tomato cages so they will grow up instead of out.

SALAD BURNET
(*Poterium sanguisorba*)

Hardiness: Zones 4 to 8
Exposure: Sun
Some Companions: Sorrel, lettuce, arugula
Primary Means of Spreading: Seeds
Aggressiveness: Moderate
Flowering Time: Late spring

The juice of salad burnet, a Eurasian native naturalized in North America, was once used to stop blood flow from cuts. But it is the mild flavor of the foliage, available for harvest spring, summer, fall, and even winter, that brings this plant into modern gardens. The leaves, which grow in a basal rosette, have up to twelve dark green, oval, toothed leaflets per compound leaf, which contrasts prettily with lettuce in a salad bowl. Their mild flavor takes on a hint of cucumber when used in herbal vinegar. In summer, the plant erects

2-foot-tall flower stalks with tiny flowers clustered in round balls. When mature and dried, the seedpods can be used in dried arrangements. By that time, they have are likely to have shed enough seed to produce an abundance of new seedlings. Move them to convenient places, spacing them about 1 foot apart.

Any well-drained garden soil is likely to work well. Salad burnet grows best if irrigated in dry weather.

GARDEN SORREL
(*Rumex acetosa*)

Hardiness: Zones 4 to 9
Exposure: Sun
Some Companions: Salad burnet, lettuce, spinach, arugula
Primary Means of Spreading: Creeping stems and seeds
Aggressiveness: Aggressive
Flowering Time: Summer

Sorrel leaves, with a lemony flavor delicious in mixed green salads, sauces, and soups, can be hard to find in the grocery store. But sorrel is easily grown and especially free-spirited. A single plant can spread into a colony, enough to supply your family and friends. Garden sorrel, a Eurasian native naturalized in North America, produces basal clusters of 6- to 12-inch-tall arrow-head-shaped leaves. Occasional runners can extend some distance from the mother plant, sprouting new leafy clusters as they grow. In summer, garden sorrel sends up 4-foot-high clusters of tiny insect-pollinated flowers that mature into attractive red-flushed winged seeds, useful in large flower arrangements. Extra seeds will spin to the ground and develop into new plants.

Sorrel grows in almost any soil, spreading most vigorously where there is abundant fertility and moisture. Pull or dig up unwanted offshoots and cut back immature seed stalks to reduce excessive spread.

BLACKBERRIES AND RASPBERRIES
(*Rubus* spp.)

Hardiness: Zones 3, 4, or 5 to 9
Exposure: Sun
Some Companions: Strawberries
Primary Means of Spreading: Creeping stems or tip sprouts
Aggressiveness: Moderate to aggressive
Flowering Time: Spring or summer

Most blackberries and raspberries are alike in growing into thickets and bearing fruit on canes (upright stems) that are two years old. They have handsome three-, five- or seven-parted compound leaves and clusters of white flowers in spring. Beyond this point, there are many differences. Raspberries produce delicate coreless berries of yellow, red, purple, or black in summer and fall. Black raspberries have waxy blue canes that emerge upright, then cascade to the ground. Where the tips touch the soil or are lightly buried, they will root and sprout into new plants, thus hopscotching across the garden. Blackberries, which bear black berries with a small core, usually ripen in summer. Most blackberries and also red raspberries spread by sprouting upright stems, called suckers, on horizontally spreading roots. Purple raspberries, hybrids between black and red raspberries, will spread using both methods.

Provide fertile, well-drained soil and good air circulation, but avoid windy locations. You can prevent unruly thickets and increase berry size by vigorously removing thin and weak canes in spring and cutting back old canes after fruiting. Most blackberries and raspberries benefit from trellising to organize the canes and keep them upright.

133

CHAPTER 8:
headstrong herb gardens

Flowers and vegetables are not the only plants capable of spreading on their own through a free-spirited garden. A crazy quilt of aromatic herbs can sweep into plaited patterns and prance around on self-sown seedlings. Unlike modern-day annuals and many of the finely bred perennials, most herbs remain closely linked to their wild ancestors, and many still grow wild somewhere in the world. While making the transition to cultivation, most have retained not only the aromatic essences that make them dear to the human heart but also a self-serving free-spirited nature. Only a few—seedless garlic and French tarragon, for instance— have lost their ability to reproduce freely.

An herbal cottage garden mixes self-seeding and creeping plants with other edibles and useful flowers.

Quite a few Eurasian herbs such as common yarrow and mint have escaped to grow wild across the American countryside, a testimony to free-spirited abilities that border on being bullying. Like any naturalized alien—useful or not—they can pose a threat to the unique native species they displace. From a practical perspective, you may want to avoid aggressive species in small gardens. In large gardens, try to contain the most vigorous so they won't break free and contaminate other gardens or wild areas.

Bronze fennel, in the center, develops a taproot best left undisturbed.

The way herbs scamper across the garden varies and depends, to a large extent, on their family relationships. Among the friskiest creepers are members of the mint family, including assorted mints, wild marjoram, and mother-of-thyme, which bolt through the garden on horizontal stems. Peppermint and spearmint lead the lot in aggressiveness, using fast-growing square-stemmed stolons to colonize as much as 3 feet or more of new ground a year. Mother-of-thyme, actually a low-growing shrub, sends out horizontal woody stems that root as they go and sprout upright branches clothed in small, fragrant leaves.

A much different strategy is employed by herbs in the Umbelliferae or carrot family including dill, fennel, angelica, chervil, and caraway. They tend to grow deep taproots that never creep and even resist transplanting once beyond a tiny seedling size. Instead these herbs hop around the garden using seeds. Produced by the dozens in umbrella-shaped clusters of tiny flowers, many of the seeds are aromatic and most are likely to self-sow.

Hundreds of different herbs are appropriate for an herb garden: any and all plants used in cuisine, crafts, dyeing, medicine, and decoration now or in the past. History plays a big role in herbal traditions, especially for Eurasian herbs, which can be traced from ancient Greek and Roman herbals, through Europe, and to the American colonies.

Centuries of experimentation—successful and fanciful—give herbs such as the following a rich heritage of lore and legend.

Orris root iris (*Iris pallida*), named after the Greek goddess of the rainbow, was used by Greeks and Romans for perfume. It was not the flowers, as one might imagine, but the fleshy creeping rhizomes that were valued. Still used today, the rhizomes are dried to release a soft aroma of violets and are chipped or ground to use as a potpourri fixative or fragrance stabilizer.

Some herbs hail from Asia including perilla or shiso (*Perilla frutescens*), a mint-flavored plant for flavoring tempura and sushi. A tender annual with purple or green leaves, it looks like a blend between large-leaved basil and coleus. Generous spikes of small white flowers produce an abundance of seeds likely to return for a command performance next year.

Native herbs from the western hemisphere may not be enriched with deep-seated lore but are valuable additions to the garden anyway. Nasturtiums, native to South America, have peppery-flavored round leaves and tender spicy flowers of red, yellow, and orange. They are at home in salads and herbal vinegars. The plump seeds self-sow lightly and can be seen naturalized in San Francisco.

As with other free-spirited gardens, containing these head-

A sundial marks the center of Mary Versfelt's herb garden.

strong herbs in a garden with strong bones provides comforting structure and interest year-round.

An Old-Fashioned Four-Square

Herbs cluster amid flowers and other edibles in the charming free-spirited herbal cottage garden of Mary Versfelt of Houston, Texas. An avid cook and longtime gardener who has flexed her green thumb in Iran, England, Turkey, Israel, Argentina, Wyoming, and Oklahoma, Versfelt encourages free-spirited spreading and the bounty that it brings.

Versfelt enjoys fragrant-flowered nicotiana that was planted by the birds late one summer and provides heavenly evening fragrances for most of the autumn. Self-sowing German chamomile comes and goes on its own schedule—arising from fall to early spring, blooming (and being used for tea), then setting seed and fading away as summer basil takes its place. Violets, originally used as an edging, appear everywhere. Amaryllis, a tender bulb that symbolized splendid beauty in the Victorian language of flowers, spreads rowdily with multiplying bulblets.

These and others in a casual collection of interesting herbs are not forced into a preconceived design but are allowed to grow where conditions are ideal. Many have found their own favorite places, arising from self-sown seeds or spreading to find an ideal niche. The garden form and sense of design comes from the traditional four-square structure, a plan originating in medieval times and

An artistic rendering of grass blades adorns one perimeter raised bed, filled with edible-flowered calendulas in Mary Versfelt's garden.

138

used continually to the present. To make a four-square, an ordinary square garden is traversed by two perpendicular walks to section it into four square beds. The walks allow for easy access in wet weather, soil that is free from compression underfoot, and a simple but elegant garden structure.

Versfelt's garden consumes most of her 60-foot-square backyard and looks particularly lovely when viewed from a second-story window. It is enclosed by a 7-foot-tall board-on-board fence, which ensures privacy, gives portions of the garden shady relief from the hot afternoon sun, and supports climbing roses, trellised purple hyacinth beans, and clusters of pots brimming with herbs and tropicals. Perimeter beds filled with flowers line the fence and nearby garage. A small plot of lawn provides a graceful green carpet between house and garden, while many antique terra-cotta pots of herbs such as sage and tarragon crowd the back patio.

Each of the four herb beds is 10 by 10 feet square, contained and raised with 4 by 4 rot-resistant timbers. The raised beds sharpen soil drainage, a necessity if herbs are to withstand onslaughts of Gulf Coast rain. The stiff native gumbo soil is lightened with abundant organic matter, most of which is created in an extensive composting system hidden behind the garage.

The 2-foot-wide brick walks are guarded by potted rosemary, which stand like sentries on either side of the garden entrance. An antique sundial is placed in the dead center of the garden. Each bed also has a centerpiece—tall tripods dripping with sweet peas or pole bean vines, a potted bay tree, or a large potted lemon verbena shrub. Pots of scented geraniums and thymes plus international folk art—an Indonesian whirligig, an antique goose, and birds nesting in a gourd—await discovery in nooks and crannies around the garden.

Versfelt finds the Houston growing season has a different pulse than colder climates, but she still manages to grow many of the same herbs. Hardy herbs like thyme and tarragon that easily withstand Chicago

Mary Versfelt gathers fresh flowers from the garden.

139

winters may falter in hot, humid southern climates. She keeps them mostly in pots, where excellent soil drainage and brisk air circulation encourage them to keep going. Chives, which go dormant during winter in the North, die back to the ground and rest during Houston summers. From October through December, Houston's cool, mild weather encourages the emergence of self-sown seedlings of cool-season herbs like borage, mustard, chervil, nasturtiums, dill, German chamomile, and cilantro, which would sprout in spring in northern climates. All of these self-sowers are allowed to grow, flower, and set seed. Their new generations might appear anywhere that Versfelt hasn't been busy digging and reorganizing.

Amaryllis multiplies in Mary Versfelt's Texas garden.

140

In winter, temperatures occasionally drop down into the teens, so tender herbs like basil, lemon verbena, and scented geraniums must be covered or they will be lost. Most of the cool-season self-sowers, however, survive this brief chill. Come the hot, sticky Houston summer, when northern herb gardens are just awaking, they fade.

Among the more successful creeping perennials is mother-of-thyme, which happily cascades over a retaining timber into the nearby walk. Wild marjoram spreads at will, regardless of summer heat or winter cold. St. John's wort, a medicinal herb, creeps and carries on through the heat nicely but has never bloomed.

Lemon grass (*Cymbopogon citratus*), a warm-climate herb from southern India, has intensely citrus-scented foliage ideal for Asian cuisine, curries, sauces, teas, and vinegars. It produces a clump of stiff, upright grassy leaves several feet high that expand outward on short rhizomes where conditions are hot and humid enough for its liking. In Houston, lemon grass survives frost with heavy mulch, but any farther north it should be potted and brought indoors for the winter.

Society garlic (*Tulbaghia violacea*), a tender bulb from South Africa, has multiplying bulbs that form expanding clumps. Pink-lavender balls of small flowers appear in spring and fall, standing over onion-flavored foliage that may be decoratively variegated. The leaves can be used like chives and remain evergreen in frost-free climates but must be potted and brought indoors in cooler climates.

Altogether, this four-square herb garden offers free-spirited abundance, beauty, and productivity in a climate made difficult by heat and humidity.

Self-Sowing Companion Plants at the National Herb Garden

The National Herb Garden, part of the National Arboretum in Washington, D.C., is one of the most beautiful and elaborate public herb gardens in the country. Walks meander by theme gardens—medicinal and culinary herbs, collections of salvias, and, for the free-spirited gardener, beds of old-fashioned roses. These roses billow into large shrubs or ramble up trellises, flowering profusely in May, then falling quiet as they develop ruby rose hips, which add tartness and vitamin C to herbal teas.

Even after the roses fade, this garden abounds with color from free-spirited self-sowing annuals that rejoice in the moist, fertile

Larkspurs and peony-flowered poppies bloom in abundance at the National Herb Garden.

141

Madalene Hill's raised beds of pea gravel improve moisture drainage and herb health.

soil. Abundant self-sowing is encouraged, says curator Jim Adams. Flowers are allowed to bloom and go to seed; they are seldom removed before the seed is ripe and the pods are dry enough to let the seeds fall free. The browning stems fade into the background as new self-sowing flowers and herbs come on.

Larkspurs (see Chapter 3) stretch up airy spires of blue and pink flowers in late May and June, peaking as the roses fade. Peony-flowered poppies do the same, springing up in any open cracks and crevices to flower in pink, peach, or red in mid-May. The blossoms linger for three to four weeks, then develop into plump, waxy blue-green pods that age elegantly to deep brown.

Sweet annie artemisia, an apple-scented annual once planted in the fragrance and medicinal gardens, now has expanded its territory and grows through many of the gardens. Fluffy, finely divided foliage is borne on plants that stretch up on stems to 10 feet high. The vivid greenery turns attractive golden hues in fall. Plants are topped with loose clusters of yellow flowers in late summer. The flowers develop into hundreds of tiny seeds, which spread like dust across open soil nearby and can emerge aggressively. A native of Eurasia and North Africa, sweet annie has used this strategy to naturalize in North America. In the garden,

Adams finds it to be an ideal late summer and fall filler, covering up where spring- and early summer-blooming plants have been cut back.

Managing these free-spirited herbs is easy. If they grow overly crowded or begin to stifle roses and other herbs nearby, they are edited or pulled out until harmony is restored.

Mediterranean Herbs in Coastal California

Many popular herbs—including free spirits like thyme, creeping rosemary, and oregano, for instance—hail from the Mediterranean, the area bordering the Mediterranean Sea that is famous for its abundant sun, long dry spells, and lean soils. Native Mediterranean herbs tend to grow slowly but steadily and have moisture-conserving foliage—small, needlelike, or leathery. The foliage also is rich in fragrant essential oils, which have little appeal for most herbivorous creatures, so the plants are seldom troubled by pests, rabbits, and other browsers.

Along the California coast, from San Diego to San Francisco and beyond, the United States has its own Mediterranean climate, a region where Mediterranean herbs make a natural transition from Old World to New World. Because temperatures seldom drop to freezing, creeping rosemary, which dies when temperatures fall below 20° F, can spread a foot a year, forming a handsome carpet of aromatic needled greenery.

The area boasts a few native American herbs of note. Creeping *Artemisia ludoviciana*, parent of 'Silver King' artemisia, may be found growing wild. So may self-sowing San Luis purple sage (*Salvia leucophylla*), a gray-leaved shrub with spikes bearing pink, blue, or purple flowers. It is both drought tolerant and allelopathic, able to release chemicals that discourage the growth of nearby vegetation.

According to Chris Dunn, longtime California gardener and co-owner of Herban Gardens near San Diego, most herbs, native or not, will self-sow here. Volunteer basil seedlings, for instance, can sprout after a week of warm weather. If they've unwisely arisen in winter, they could just as quickly die back on an unexpected frosty night. Self-sown basil seedlings, particularly offspring from special cultivars with purple or ruffled leaves or special flavorings like 'Sweet Dani' lemon basil, don't often resemble their parents and may be less desirable. In contrast, Dunn finds dill, cilantro, chives, and garlic chives, which grow well despite a little chilling, are particularly productive self-seeding herbs suitable for growing year-round.

Horticultural Hints

There are hundreds of different herbs you can grow—something for every environment—but many of the most common culinary favorites have two nonnegotiable needs. They require well-drained soil and sun.

Most Mediterranean, culinary, and silver-leaved herbs prefer full sun, at least six hours a day. In hot climates like Houston, however, even sun-loving species do better with light afternoon shade in summer. If your herb garden has less than six hours of sun a day, you can grow shade-tolerant herbs such as parsley and basil or turn to light shade–loving plants such as angelica, mint, sweet woodruff, and sweet cicely. Starting with the right plants for the light exposure is vital to growing healthy plants that are capable of reproducing and expanding.

Loose sandy soil, slightly sloped beds, and gardens created in raised beds or immediately behind retaining walls tend to be well-drained. It's not always safe to assume drainage is adequate, however, without first trying a simple drainage test. When the soil is dry, dig a hole 1 foot deep and 2 feet wide. Fill the hole with water and note how long it takes to percolate out. For herbs like thyme and rosemary that need sharp drainage, the water should drain out in less than thirty minutes. If it takes more than thirty minutes and less than four hours, the soil is well suited for herbs like basil and parsley, which prefer average to rich soil. Soil that takes longer than four hours to drain runs the gamut between moist and waterlogged and might serve for mint or wintercress, but little else.

Madalene Hill, herb lecturer, writer, and scholar, has found the survival rate of herbs in her Festival Hill, Texas, garden has skyrocketed with a technique that dramatically improves moisture drainage. A bed

A sculpted cat stands watch over the garden and serves as a focal point.

raised several inches high is topped with 2 or 3 inches of pea gravel, which keeps the top of the roots and emerging herb shoots dry and discourages diseases and plant losses. Where drought can be a problem, you can run a soaker hose under the gravel layer and irrigate below the soil surface when conditions get dry. (For more on gravel gardening, see Chapter 6.)

Once situated in a suitable site, herbs that spread by creeping may need occasional restraining to keep them loosely within bounds. Bossy spreaders like mint are best restricted in contained beds or sunken bottomless nursery pots, and not allowed the freedom of the open garden. Plants such as thyme and oregano that root as they creep can be trimmed back with a shovel. Cut off new growth at an advantageous point and scoop the offshoots up, roots and all. This allows you to uproot entire sections, leaving few to no bits and pieces to resprout. You can take the rooted divisions to plant in pots, give to friends, or harvest for the kitchen.

If creeping herbs excessively soften a once-structured planting plan, you can dig up and divide the plants. Add some extra organic matter to the soil, then replant young sections in an orderly design. They will have a new beginning and will grow nicely for at least several more years before being ready for another revision.

Adding Character and Structure

Some free-spirited herbs are small in stature and have modest-looking leaves and flowers. They are loved more for what they can do than for the drama of their appearance. When they are given the freedom to ramble and intermingle, minor variations in color and texture can be lost from afar as, for instance, thymes blur beneath oreganos. To add distinction, without limiting free-spirited spreading, let them ramble amid a strongly structured garden. Instead of painstakingly manhandling herbs into clipped geometric patterns, as is done in formal herb gardens, substitute built elements—networks of paths, geometric raised beds, and interesting accessories for labor-intensive clipped knots and edgings.

The four-square garden, described on page 138, is a perfect example of structure with free-spirited freedom. Another easy design uses matching semicircular, rectangular, triangular, or square beds on either side of a central walk or patio area. For a central focal point, set dramatic sculpture, keepsakes, reflecting pools, or potted plants between the beds. Edge both gardens with a low hedge of stay-put shrubbery such as 'Green Gem' boxwood or English lavender. Include marching lines or clusters of annuals for formal color that duplicates the outlines of the garden. Within this stable framework, let your herbs mingle. Reserve the front of the garden for low creepers and the back for taller self-seeders.

No matter what the design, built elements help to give the herb garden character. To create an old-fashioned ambience, for example, begin by making garden walks of old brick. Salvaged worn and faded from old houses or streets, it has a charm well suited to herbs. Other old-fashioned elements—beeskeps (woven baskets once used to house domestic bees), wattle fences woven with young branches, and even antique urns or pumps—can add to the historical ambience.

Self-seeding chives bloom beside bearded iris.

Glossary of Creeping and Self-Sowing Herbs

Herbs can bring a wealth of flavor, fragrance, and history to a productive free-spirited garden. Profiles of their uses and spreading techniques, along with growing tips, are detailed in the following glossary.

WOOLY YARROW

(Achillea tomentosa)

Hardiness: Zones 4 to 10
Exposure: Sun
Some Companions: Winter savory, creeping rosemary, lamb's ears
Primary Means of Spreading: Creeping stems
Aggressiveness: Limited to moderate
Flowering Time: Summer

A mat of finely cut gray-haired foliage makes a handsome edging for an herb garden. In summer, Wooly Yarrow sparkles with small flat-topped heads of yellow flowers that can reach a foot high. Cut them for arrangements, which helps keep the foliage looking attractive and encourages vegetative spreading. The genus *Achillea* is named in honor of the almost invincible Greek warrior, Achilles, who used yarrows to dress his soldier's wounds.

Wooly yarrow, a Eurasian native, grows best in well-drained, average to lean soils. In overly moist soils, it can be prone to rotting.

'Licorice Blue' anise hyssop bears blue-purple flower spikes and anise-scented leaves.

ANISE HYSSOP

(Agastache foeniculum)

Hardiness: Zones 4 to 8
Exposure: Sun to partial sun
Some Companions: Bee balm, borage, catmint
Primary Means of Spreading: Seeds
Aggressiveness: Moderate
Flowering Time: Summer

This midwestern herb lacks the lore of Eurasian species but makes up for it in fragrance. Its strongly licorice-scented leaves make interesting herb teas and garnishes for fruit salads and desserts. Anise hyssop has opposite toothed leaves and bright spikes of blue or purple flowers that reach 2 to 4 feet tall. The flowers attract bees and butterflies, colorful additions to the garden. A member of the mint family, this plant stands apart as a nonmotile clump former. It qualifies as free spirited, however, because it seeds freely. A biennial or short-lived perennial, anise hyssop spreads abundantly enough to merit use in prairie as well as herb gardens.

Provide full sun or light shade and average to modestly fertile, well-drained soil.

COMMON CHIVES

(Allium schoenoprasum)

Hardiness: Zones 4 to 9
Exposure: Sun
Some Companions: Lady's mantle, bronze fennel, purple basil
Primary Means of Spreading: Seeds and multiplying bulbs
Aggressiveness: Moderate to aggressive
Flowering Time: Spring

Common chives are attractive and easy-care herbs. Onion-flavored tubular leaves arise from slowly expanding clumps of mini-bulbs. Chive leaves, cut off at the base, can be sprinkled on potatoes with sour cream or mixed in salads, soups, burgers, dips, and butters. In late spring, flowering stems sprout globular clusters of small lavender flowers, wonderful for making herbal vinegar or garnishing salads or soups. Any flowers left to mature are likely to self-sow, sometimes heavily. A native to Eurasia, chives may have first been used in the Orient and caught on in Europe after the time of Marco Polo.

Provide rich, moist but well-drained soil. Although common chives may survive in warm climates, they perform best where winter is cold enough for a period of dormancy.

GARLIC CHIVES

(Allium tuberosum)

Hardiness: Zones 5 to 9
Exposure: Sun
Some Companions: Parsley, lovage, perilla
Primary Means of Spreading: Creeping stems and seeds
Aggressiveness: Moderate to aggressive
Flowering Time: Summer

Here is a garlic-flavored counterpart to common chives. The flat upright foliage, which grows in clumps on creeping rhizomes, can reach 2 feet tall. While common chives flower early in the growing season, garlic chives produce fragrant white flowers later in the summer. If allowed to set seeds, garlic chives may self-seed even more aggressively than common chives. With a birthplace in Southeast Asia, garlic chives (also called Oriental chives) are commonly used in Chinese and related cuisine. They can be substituted for common chives in almost any recipe for a hint of garlic. Try garlic chives chopped and sprinkled in soup broth or on eggs just before serving.

Like common chives, garlic chives thrive easily in rich, moist but well-drained soil.

DILL
(Anethum graveolens)

Hardiness: Annual
Exposure: Sun
Some Companions: Parsley, calendula, nasturtium, German chamomile
Primary Means of Spreading: Seeds
Aggressiveness: Limited to moderate
Flowering Time: Summer and fall

Dill, which has deliciously flavored, ferny foliage and seeds, is a handsome and quick-growing annual. The threadlike leaves—called dill weed—can be harvested lightly at any time but become less abundant after flowering. Dill weed is marvelous in dips, on vegetables or chicken, and in herb butters, herbal vinegars, and more. Dill plants quickly stretch up tall and slim to reach about 3 feet high and produce flat-topped clusters of yellow flowers. If allowed to mature, the flowers produce flattened white-ribbed dark seeds wonderful for dill pickles, breads, and soups. Seeds allowed to scatter to the ground often produce volunteer seedlings. A native of Southwest Asia, dill has escaped and naturalized in parts of North America and Europe. Well loved throughout history,

dill has been used for settling stomachs, casting spells, and biblical tithing.

Dill grows easily in well-drained soil of modest to average fertility. Direct-sow seeds, firming them on top of the soil.

ANGELICA
(Angelica archangelica)

Hardiness: Zones 3 to 7
Exposure: Sun to partial shade
Some Companions: Sweet woodruff, lady's mantle, chervil
Primary Means of Spreading: Seeds
Aggressiveness: Limited
Flowering Time: Summer

Angelica is a dynamite architectural plant, strutting huge, dark green, divided leaves and broad umbels of small, greenish white flowers that reach up to 6 feet high. It is likely to grow as a biennial, flowering its second year and then dying. Any fresh seed it produces can self-sow and develop into replacement plants (although older packaged seed is hard to coax to germinate). Possessing a mild anise flavor, the young stems historically have been stewed or candied and the aromatic seeds used as a sweet spice. Native to Eurasia, the botanical name *Angelica* reflects associations with things angelic. Angelica was believed to prevent plague and also used for flavoring liqueurs.

Angelica likes living well in rich, fertile, and evenly moist soil. Because angelica has a taproot, you should attempt to transplant only young seedlings without deep roots.

CHERVIL
(Anthriscus cerefolium)

Hardiness: Annual
Exposure: Partial shade
Some Companions: Sweet woodruff, wild ginger, angelica
Primary Means of Spreading: Seeds

Aggressiveness: Limited to moderate
Flowering Time: Summer

A French favorite, chervil looks like a narrow-leaved parsley but actually is a short-lived annual that thrives during cool growing seasons. Plants develop into graceful low mounds of fine foliage, then stretch up 1 or 2 feet high, producing spreading umbrella-shaped clusters of tiny white flowers. If allowed to complete seed production, they can self-sow to replace faded stands in fall or the next spring. A Eurasian native popular in European kitchens since the Middle Ages, chervil has begun to find a place in American gardens. The delicately anise-flavored leaves can be used in cream sauces, with eggs, on chicken, and with other mild-flavored foods that allow the subtle flavor to shine through.

For a first crop, direct-sow seeds in spring or fall, covering them very lightly. Provide moist and fertile soil.

SILVER KING ARTEMISIA
(Artemisia ludoviciana var. albula 'Silver King')

Hardiness: Zones 5 to 9
Exposure: Sun
Some Companions: Yarrow, fennel, purple basil, purple perilla
Primary Means of Spreading: Rhizomes
Aggressiveness: Aggressive
Flowering Time: Late summer

While most *Artemisia* species hail from Eurasia, this species is distinctly American and worth bragging about. With narrow silver foliage on upright stems 2 to 3 feet high, it grows into a bushy thicket of silver useful in herb or perennial gardens (see Chapter 2). Other artemisia species have been used medicinally and as pest repellents but this plant is primarily ornamental. The foliage makes a strong silver accent

149

and contrasts with green- and bronze-leaved herbs. It also is delightful in fresh and dried flower arrangements and wreaths. 'Silver King' is among the friskiest of free-spirited perennials. Underground rhizomes can tunnel for several feet from their origin to send up new plantlets, making for endless surprises. To avoid unpleasant disruptions, isolate the plant in its own bed, plant it in an underground container, or put it with other strong spreaders and let them duke it out.

Provide well-drained soil of limited to moderate fertility for best growth.

Borage has furry stems and edible star-shaped blue flowers.

BORAGE
(Borago officinalis)

Hardiness: Annual
Exposure: Sun
Some Companions: Basil, arugula, German chamomile, anise hyssop, catmint
Primary Means of Spreading: Seeds
Aggressiveness: Aggressive
Flowering Time: Summer

A unique plant, borage has succulent furry leaves with a cool mild flavor. The clear blue, star-shaped flowers are edible or good to dry for potpourri. Ancient Romans combined borage with wine to treat heartbreaking sorrow, and later it was thought to help fevers and sore throats. Today borage is found in salads, vinegars, and juiced health drinks. A fast and luxuriant grower, borage swells from a seedling to 2 or 3 feet high, often needing support to keep from sprawling. The taproot sinks deep and prevents transplanting once beyond a tiny stage. Flowers require cross-pollination. If allowed to seed freely, borage can produce legions of seedlings for the next several years.

Provide well-drained soil of light to average fertility. Pinching frequently will help the plant remain self-supporting.

ROMAN CHAMOMILE
(Chamaemelum nobile syn. Anthemis nobilis)

Hardiness: Zones 3 to 10
Exposure: Sun to light shade
Some Companions: Thyme, lovage, coneflowers
Primary Means of Spreading: Creeping stems
Aggressiveness: Moderate
Flowering Time: Summer

This creeping perennial has low-growing stems that root as they spread and feathery, finely divided, aromatic foliage. Once used for carpeting the herbal lawns and fragrant garden seats of European aristocracy, Roman chamomile is today more common as a sunny ground cover for a bank or dry rocky area, and sometimes in a miniherbal lawn beside a patio or around a sculpture. During summer, Roman chamomile sends up inch-wide daisylike flowers with yellow centers and white outer rays. They can reach 1 foot tall and are charming to dry and add to potpourri. Native from Western Europe to North Africa, Roman chamomile is occasionally found escaped in North America.

Plant nursery plants, divisions, or seedlings in well-drained lean soil. Avoid walking on it excessively, which can damage the plant.

CILANTRO
(Coriandrum sativum)

Hardiness: Annual
Exposure: Sun
Some Companions: Dill, parsley, tomatoes
Primary Means of Spreading: Seeds
Aggressiveness: Moderate
Flowering Time: Summer

The same plant that yields cilantro—pungent, often finely divided foliage that people tend to love or hate—also produces warmly aromatic seeds used as the sweet spice coriander. Although native to southern Europe, this plant's distinctive flavor has earned a devoted following in Asian, Indian, North African, Mexican, and Caribbean cuisine. Spring-planted cilantro usually bolts in summer, stretching up to 3 feet tall and bearing flat-topped clusters of white to pale pink flowers. If allowed to mature, these will yield flavorful coriander seeds for the kitchen and self-sowing. Perhaps free-spirited seeding is the reason ancient Chinese believed coriander represented immortality.

Cilantro grows best in cool, mild weather and can be planted shortly before the last spring frost for an extended foliage harvest. Provide moist, well-drained soil.

Bronze Fennel
(Foeniculum vulgare 'Purpurescens')

Hardiness: Zones 5 to 9
Exposure: Sun
Some Companions: Artemisia, lamb's ears, nasturtium, catmint
Primary Means of Spreading: Seeds
Aggressiveness: Moderate to aggressive
Flowering Time: Summer

Bronze fennel, with fronds of feathery purple to purple-green leaves, is popular in herb gardens for its anise-flavored leaves and seeds. It also is being discovered by flower gardeners, who find it makes a dashing dark contrast with silver or green foliage. Fennel stretches up on sheathed stems to 3 feet tall, or even taller, then opens flat-topped clusters of tiny yellow flowers. The flowers mature into dark dry pods, bearing flavorful seeds that self-sow easily and can colonize an expanding swath of the garden as years go by. Chopped fennel leaves are delicious with carrots and fish, while the seeds can be blended into sausage or baked goods. Beloved by ancient Greeks and Romans, fennel was prescribed for dieting, eye problems, building strength and courage, and protection against evil.

A native of southern Europe and the Mediterranean, fennel is able to grow in a wide range of conditions from lean well-drained soil to moist fertile soil. Seedlings quickly develop a deep taproot and are not easily moved once past a very young age. Once growing strongly, fennel tends to be drought tolerant.

Sweet Woodruff
(Galium odoratum)

Hardiness: Zones 3 to 8
Exposure: Shade
Some Companions: Angelica, chervil, hostas, azaleas, variegated Solomon's seal, mayapple
Primary Means of Spreading: Creeping and prostrate stems and seeds
Aggressiveness: Moderate to aggressive
Flowering Time: Spring

Sweet woodruff is one of the few herbs that revels in shade and rich moist soil, the same conditions as many woodland wildflowers (see Chapter 4). But because it can be a feisty spreader—advancing steadily on underground stems as well as prostrate stems that root where they touch the ground and self-sown seedlings—it's best if you avoid turning the plant loose in a pristine woods where it will compete with the woodland natives. Sweet woodruff reaches only 6 inches high, spreading horizontally to blanket the soil with bright green leaves held in beautiful whorling clusters. Tiny star-shaped white flowers cover the plant in spring. If you let handfuls of sweet woodruff dry, they take on a pleasant vanillalike odor, once enjoyed stuffed into mattresses or strewn on the floor of musty castles.

Native to Eurasia and North Africa, sweet woodruff grows easily in all but the warmest American climates. Give it space to spread and water during dry weather to prevent premature dormancy.

German chamomile blooms beside a wall covered with ivy.

German Chamomile
(Matricaria recutita)

Hardiness: Annual
Exposure: Sun
Some Companions: Calendula, nasturtium, arugula, mustard
Primary Means of Spreading: Seeds
Aggressiveness: Limited
Flowering Time: Summer and fall

This short-lived annual is the sweet-flavored cousin of Roman chamomile (*Chamaemelum nobile*). The apple-scented, yellow-centered daisylike flowers make a calming herbal tea that some people believe helps them sleep but may not agree with people allergic to ragweed. German chamomile grows into little bushes about 2½ feet high, clad in threadlike foliage. Any flowers left to mature will produce tiny dustlike gray seeds that can spread far and wide if they blow around the garden. Once plants run to seed, their days are numbered, but you can count on new plants arriving when the weather is right. A native of northern Europe, German chamomile bears seeds that germinate best at 60° F, thriving in spring and again in fall where weather is mild.

Direct-sow German chamomile seeds on light well-drained soil, sprinkling them on the soil surface without covering them.

Lemon Balm
(Melissa officinalis)

Hardiness: Zones 4 to 9
Exposure: Sun to light shade
Some Companions: Mints, anise hyssop, bee balm
Primary Means of Spreading: Creeping stems and seeds
Aggressiveness: Aggressive
Flowering Time: Summer and fall

151

The most wonderful lemon fragrance arises from the scallop-edged oval leaves of this plant, which quickly swells from a seedling into a thick bush 2 or 3 feet high. Use leafy sprigs in iced tea, on fruit salads or desserts, or as a garnish for fish or chicken dishes. In Europe, lemon balm has been well researched and is used medicinally as a sedative and more. Like others in the mint family, lemon balm has distinctive square stems but is not inclined to run rampant through the garden on creeping stems. Instead it produces abundant seeds and hoards of seedlings. In summer, spikes of small white flowers arise and should be cut back to prevent excessive spread.

A native of southern Europe, lemon balm has escaped in eastern North America. While lemon balm will grow on average soils, it thrives in rich, moist soil.

MINT
(Mentha spp.)

Hardiness: Zones 4 to 9
Exposure: Shade to sun
Some Companions: Lemon balm, angelica, sweet woodruff
Primary Means of Spreading: Creeping stems and seeds
Aggressiveness: Aggressive
Flowering Time: Summer

There are dozens of different kinds of mints, but some general assumptions can be made about most of them. They have square stems and opposite leaves endowed with fragrant essential oils, most of which are delightful. In addition to peppermint and spearmint flavorings, there are lemon, apple, pineapple, and other essences quite enjoyable for teas, fruit salads, chicken, lamb, or fish. Mints also share an appetite for running through the garden on creeping stems that sprout rooted shoots everywhere they go. Many mint species, called promiscuous by jovial botanists, can freely cross-pollinate and interbreed to produce a unique blend of hybrid offspring. According to mythology, mint actually is one of Pluto's lovers, changed into a mint plant. It has been used by ancients as an aphrodesiac, wine flavoring, and breath freshener—the latter still prevailing today. Conquering Roman armies carried spearmint to England, and British colonists transported it to North America. Today mints are used for cuisine, cosmetics, cleaning supplies, jellies, salads, vinegars, desserts, and more.

Peppermint (*Mentha* x *piperita*), a hybrid, has oval leaves on stems often tinged with purple. It may grow to be 3 feet high. Although it produces many lavender flowers in crowded clusters at the ends of stems, they are sterile.

Spearmint (*M. spicata*), which grows about 30 inches high, has petioleless leaves and a characteristic sharp minty odor. The lavender, pink, or white flowers arrive in summer and can produce seeds. Native to Eurasia, spearmint has naturalized in parts of the eastern United States.

Apple mint (*M. suaveolens*), has slightly fuzzy leaves with a fruity flavor and fragrance. The flowers are pink or white. A handsome variegated form is called pineapple mint.

Provide mints with highly organic, moist soil, and water during dry weather. Contain mints in isolated beds or sunken containers if interplanting with other herbs or plants.

SWEET CICELY
(Myrrhis odorata)

Hardiness: Zones 3 to 8
Exposure: Light shade
Some Companions: Sweet woodruff, angelica, contained mints
Primary Means of Spreading: Seeds
Aggressiveness: Moderate to aggressive

Sweet cicely is one of a few select shade-loving herbs and also an enthusiastic self-seeder. Lovely ferny leaves with a mild licorice scent emerge on the scene early in spring and turn a farewell burgundy before fading back to the ground in late fall. In the summer, they stretch up lofty flowering stems to 3 feet tall, bearing flowers reminiscent of Queen Anne's lace. The anise-scented immature seeds are useful in teas and baked desserts. Any seeds you miss harvesting may emerge as seedlings next year.

Provide moist but well-drained soil enriched with extra organic matter. Water during dry weather.

WILD MARJORAM OR OREGANO
(Origanum vulgare)

Hardiness: Zones 4 to 9
Exposure: Sun
Some Companions: Thyme, sage, tarragon, lavender, rosemary
Primary Means of Spreading: Creeping stems
Aggressiveness: Moderate to aggressive
Flowering Time: Summer or fall

A great variety of plants fall under this species. All share a propensity to spread on rhizomes to form matted networks. Some forms creep close to the ground while others bush up to 2 1/2 feet high.

The leaves are oval and often slightly furry. Some varieties are nearly flavorless and are grown for their handsome golden leaves or showy purple-bracted flowers used in cut flower arrangements. Other forms have wonderfully flavored foliage, cooked with meats, tomato dishes, pasta, and pizza. Once plucked to stuff into little bouquets, called nosegays, oregano was held close to the nose to protect against the evils of poor sanitation.

Oregano, a Eurasian species found in the Mediterranean, is best grown in a well-drained, even lean soil. Although it can spread aggressively, the roots are not deep and are easily moved. Yellow-leaved and variegated types can perform better in afternoon shade.

Lamb's ears spread beneath a stone bench.

LAMB'S EARS

(Stachys byzantina)

Hardiness: Zones 4 to 9
Exposure: Sun
Some Companions: Sage, artemisia, rue, catmint, lavender, fennel
Primary Means of Spreading: Creeping stems
Aggressiveness: Limited to moderate
Flowering Time: Summer

Lamb's ears have furry, elongated silver leaves that resemble their namesake. They spread on creeping stems that root as they grow to form a carpet of silver greenery. In summer, lamb's ears send up furry spikes of purple flowers that can reach 2 feet high and are lovely in fresh or dried flower arrangements. Cultivars with extra large leaves and flowerless forms are also available. Use them for contrast with bronze- or green-leaved herbs or to echo the brightness of other silver-leaved herbs like artemisia and sage. Lamb's ears are reputed to have been used to bind wounds, like an old-fashioned bandage.

Native to the arid areas around Turkey and Iran, lamb's ears grows best in lean soil with good drainage.

WILD THYME

(Thymus serpyllum)/Mother of Thyme (Thymus pulegioides or Thymus praecox subsp. articus)

Hardiness: Zones 5 to 9
Exposure: Sun
Some Companions: Winter savory, oregano, sage, creeping rosemary
Primary Means of Spreading: Creeping stems
Aggressiveness: Moderate
Flowering Time: Late spring and early summer

These species represent the more motile of the confused thyme clan. Creeping woody stems root as they grow and send out upright branches to about 6 inches high, clad in fragrant rounded or elongated leaves. In late spring or early summer, they can be covered with small spikes of purple, pink, white, or red flowers.

Vigorous European spreaders that can expand more than a foot a year, some creeping thymes have naturalized in the northeastern United States. Still believed by some romantics to be hiding places for fairies, thyme can be part of spring fairy celebrations. An ancient antiseptic, some essential oils in thyme have shown true medicinal activity. Flowers, which produce tiny and relatively unimportant seeds, attract abundant pollinators as they change from male to female to facilitate cross-pollination. The fragrant leaves, stripped off the woody stems, are wonderful cooked with meats or tomato sauces, soups, vinegars, and more, and also can be dried to add to potpourri.

Plant in well-drained to sharply drained soil. In southern climates, provide free air circulation to discourage diseases. Cut back barren or woody stems in spring to stimulate healthy young regrowth. Trim off old flowers to keep the plant tidy. If sections begin to decline, dig up and divide plants, replanting only healthy young growth.

153

Some Sources

One of the best places to
find free-spirited plants is
in your own community—
getting divisions from
friends, frequenting wildflower sales and plant
exchanges, and visiting
top-quality local nurseries
that can offer advice with
quality plants. You also can
find a great diversity of
other free-spirited plants
through mail-order nursery
specialists such as the following. Ordering from a
company close to your
home often allows you to
choose from a selection of
plants and seeds best suited
for your climate and soil
conditions.

Blossom Hill Wildflowers, W. 4084 120th
Ave., Maiden Rock, WI 54750; 800-698-
9071

Companion Plants, 7247 N. Coolville Ridge
Rd., Athens, OH 45701; 614-592-4643

Native Seeds/SEARCH, 526 N. 4th Ave.,
Tucson, AZ 85705; 520-622-5561

Niche Gardens, 1111 Dawson Rd., Chapel
Hill, NC 27516; 919-967-0078

Plant Delights Nursery, 9241 Sauls Rd.,
Raleigh, NC 27603; 919-772-4794

Plants of the Wild, P.O. Box 866, Tekoa, WA
99033; 509-284-2848

Prairie Nursery, P.O. Box 306, Westfield,
WI 53964; 608-296-3697

Seed Savers Exchange, 3076 N. Winn Rd.,
Decorah, IA 52101; 319-382-5990

Southern Exposure Seed Exchange, P.O.
Box 170, Earlysville, VA 22936; 804-973-
4703

Territorial Seed Company, P.O. Box 157,
Cottage Grove, OR 97424-0061; 541-942-
9547

Recommended Reading and References

Wild Ones Handbook. Wild Ones, P.O.
Box 23576, Milwaukee, WI 53223-0576.

Blanchan, Neltje. *Wild Flowers, An Aid to
Knowledge of Wild Flowers and Their
Insect Visitors*. New York: Doubleday,
Page, and Co., 1916.

Brennan, Georgeanne. *In the French
Kitchen Garden*. San Francisco: Chronicle
Books, 1998.

Brickell, Christopher, and Judith Zuk, eds.
*The American Horticultural Society A - Z
Encyclopedia of Garden Plants*. New
York: DK Publishing, 1997.

Burrell, C. Coleston. *A Gardener's
Encyclopedia of Wildflowers*. Emmaus,
Pa.: Rodale Press, 1997.

Jelitto, Leo, and Wilhelm Schacht. *Hardy
Herbaceous Perennials*. Portland, Ore.:
Timber Press, 1990.

Jones, Samuel Jr. and Leonard E. Foote.
Gardening with Native Wildflowers.
Portland, Ore.: Timber Press, 1990.

McClure, Susan. *Culinary Gardens from
Design to Palate*. Golden, Colo.: Fulcrum
Publishing, 1997.

McClure, Susan. *The Herb Gardener*.
Pownal, Vt.: Storey/Gardenway, 1996.

Pavord, Anna. *The New Kitchen Garden*.
New York: DK Publishing, 1996.

Phillips, Ellen, and C. Coleston Burrell.
*Rodale's Illustrated Encyclopedia of
Perennials*. Emmaus, Pa.: Rodale Press,
1993.

Phillips, Harry. *Growing and Propagating
Wildflowers*. Chapel Hill: University of
North Carolina Press, 1985.

Stein, Sara. *Noah's Garden*. Boston:
Houghton Mifflin, 1993.

Swink, Floyd, and Gerould Wilhelm. *Plants
of the Chicago Region*. Indianapolis:
Indiana Academy of Science, 1994.

154

Index

156